Hannah Arendt

In the same series

Hannah Arendt

Samantha Rose Hill

REAKTION BOOKS

For my father, Paul, who understands new beginnings.

Published by
REAKTION BOOKS LTD
Unit 32, Waterside
44–48 Wharf Road
London N1 7UX, UK

www.reaktionbooks.co.uk

First published 2021
Copyright © Samantha Rose Hill 2021

Printed and bound in Great Britain by TJ Books Ltd, Padstow, Cornwall

A catalogue record for this book is available from the British Library

ISBN 978 1 78914 379 9

Contents

Hannah Arendt, 1940s, photographed by Fred Stein.

Introduction: Understanding

We play at paste,
Till qualified for pearl,
Then drop the paste,
And deem ourself a fool.
The shapes, though, were similar,
And our new hands
Learned gem-tactics,
Practicing sands.

Emily Dickinson[1]

'What is the subject of our thought? Experience! Nothing else!'
Hannah Arendt exclaimed in 1972 at a conference on 'The Work
of Hannah Arendt', which had been organized by the Toronto
Society for the Study of Social and Political Thought. Arendt was
invited to attend the conference as a guest of honour and insisted on
participating instead.

In many ways Hannah Arendt's work is about thinking. In her
Denktagebuch (thinking journals) she asks: 'Gibt es ein Denken
das nicht Tyrannisches ist?' (Is there a way of thinking that is not
tyrannical?) At the beginning of *The Human Condition* she posits:
'What I propose, therefore, is very simple: it is nothing more than
to think what we are doing.'[2] When she covered the trial of Adolf

Eichmann in Jerusalem for the *New Yorker*, she found Eichmann lacked the capacity to engage in self-reflective thinking, to imagine the world from the perspective of another. Arendt's final work, *The Life of the Mind*, begins with a treatise on 'Thinking'.

But thinking and experience go hand-in-hand for Hannah Arendt, and there is little question that the social and political conditions of the twentieth century shaped her life and work. Born in Germany in 1906 to a well-established secular Jewish family, Arendt sensed from an early age that she was different, an outsider, a rebel or, as she would later come to say, a pariah and an outlaw. The facts of her life do not dispute this claim. Arendt was expelled from her gymnasium at fourteen for leading a protest against a teacher who offended her. When her first husband, Günther Anders, left Berlin in 1933, she stayed behind and turned their apartment into an underground stop to help communists fleeing the country. The same year, she was arrested by the Gestapo for collecting examples of anti-Semitic propaganda in the Prussian State Library. She fled to Paris where she learned French and studied Hebrew while working with Youth Aliyah to help Jewish youth emigrate to Palestine. At the age of 33 she was interned in Gurs in the south of France for five weeks before taking part in a mass escape. She emigrated to the United States in the summer of 1941, and went to work as a housekeeper to learn English before beginning to write for a number of Jewish journals. She took a job with the Conference on Jewish Relations to help Jewish families and organizations reclaim their stolen property and taught courses on European history all while writing her first major work, *The Origins of Totalitarianism*.

Her good friend the American author Mary McCarthy described her as 'a magnificent stage diva'.[3] German philosopher Hans Jonas said she had 'an intensity, an inner direction, an instinct for quality, a groping for essence, a probing for depth, which cast a magic about her'.[4] Julia Kristeva, a Bulgarian-French philosopher, wrote 'Many of Arendt's contemporaries spoke to her womanly seductiveness; those from the New York salons mused about the "Weimar flapper".'[5] The playwright Lionel Abel called her 'Hannah Arrogant'.[6] The FBI described her as 'a small, rotund, stoop shouldered woman with a crew-like haircut, masculine voice, and marvelous mind.'[7] Perhaps what is most difficult to understand about Hannah Arendt is that she was, by all accounts, *sui generis*. Absolutely incomparable.

In Hannah Arendt's youthful self-portrait *Die Schatten* (The Shadows), she describes her hunger for experience in the world as being 'trapped in a craving'. What drove her to her work from an early age was an insatiable desire to experience and understand life.[8] As she would later come to argue, the work of understanding, unlike the urge to know, requires an endless commitment to the activity of thinking; it requires one to always be ready to begin again.

In many respects Arendt became a writer by accident. She said she wrote to remember what she thought, to record what was worth remembering, and that writing was an integral part of the process of understanding. This is evidenced throughout her journals and published work, where she engaged in what she called 'thinking exercises'. In her preface to *Between Past and Future: Eight Exercises in Political Thought*, she wrote that 'thought itself arises out of incidents of living experience and must remain bound to them as the only guidepost by which to take its bearings.' For Arendt, thinking exercises were a way to engage in the work of understanding, and they were a way to break free from her education in the tradition of German philosophy.

After the burning of the Reichstag in 1933, Arendt left the world of academic philosophy to do the work of political thinking. She was appalled by how the 'professional thinkers' had been blind to the rise of National Socialism in Germany and had contributed to the Nazification of cultural and political institutions. Instead of protesting the emergence of Hitler's regime, they were carried along by the tide of history. She swore off this 'milieu' and said she'd 'never again get involved in any kind of intellectual business'.[9] The question Arendt had written in her thinking journal, 'Is there a way of thinking that is not tyrannical?' was followed by the statement: 'The question is how one can avoid swimming in the tide at all.'[10] Thinking, as an activity, does not belong to some rarefied world of professional philosophers. 'Intellectual', she said, was a hateful word. She held that everyone was capable of engaging in self-reflective critical thinking, and that doing so was necessary if one is to resist the tide of ideological thought and claim personal responsibility in the face of fascism.

Arendt did not often talk about her methodology. Her political thinking did not move from a predetermined point of analysis. She had no fixed frameworks. She was not writing in order to solve practical political problems, nor was she writing systematic philosophy, theorizing concepts like truth, beauty or the good. Her work was Socratic in spirit – dialogic, open to contradiction and always returning to the beginning. In a seminar she taught on 'The History of Political Theory' in 1955, she began by saying that concepts are not ends in themselves, but wellsprings from which we begin to do the work of thinking. The implication of this is that there cannot be something like 'the truth', because 'the truth' must constantly be rethought from the vantage point of our newest experiences.

In her essay 'Walter Benjamin' she describes this way of thinking as 'pearl diving', echoing Shakespeare's *The Tempest* (Act I, scene 2):

Full fathom five thy father lies;
Of his bones are coral made;
Those are pearls that were his eyes:
Nothing of him that doth fade,
But doth suffer a sea-change
Into something rich and strange.

Arendt's work deals with these elements of the past after they have undergone their 'sea-change'. We cannot look to the past to find analogies for the present, nor can we look to the past to find some causal, linear chain of reasoning to explain a historical event like the emergence of totalitarianism. 'Pearl diving' is a way of approaching history that is fragmentary, so that one can bring to the surface those rich and strange gems that might offer some illumination.

For Arendt, the work of thinking and understanding requires solitude. She drew a sharp distinction between the four walls of the private realm and the public space of appearances. And from an early age, there was a tension between her appetite for solitude and her desire for recognition. Even the reading of a book, she reflected, requires some degree of isolation. In order to engage in the activity of thinking, one must retreat from the harsh light of the public in order to experience the silent dialogue of thought. Arendt called this dialogue the 'two-in-one': the conversation one has with one's self. Thinking is also a process of self-understanding, a knowing with oneself. When one experiences the silent dialogue of thought, the thinking ego splits in two, and when one reappears in the world, the ego repairs itself into one. In this space of thinking, a person is able to confront their experiences, their beliefs, and what it is they think they know. Arendt said, 'The notion that there exist dangerous thoughts is mistaken for the simple reason that thinking itself is dangerous to all creeds, convictions, and opinions.'

This is not an easy task. It is no coincidence that Arendt's thinking exercises carry a connotation of danger. Experience and experiment share the same etymological root with *experiri* (to attempt), which is related to *periculum* (peril). This is perhaps what Arendt was thinking about when she said, 'There are no dangerous thoughts, thinking itself is dangerous.'[11] The activity of thinking, of coming to understand the world, has the power to unsettle everything one may believe. Thinking has the power to make us come undone.

Hannah Arendt rejected all forms of ideological thinking. She did not subscribe to a particular school of thought or philosophical doctrine. Arendt's life and work offer readers a way of thinking that teaches one how to think, rather than offering a set of arguments for what to think. As a result, many readers of Arendt have tried to place her in one political tradition or another, which is ironic since Arendt's commitment to understanding is a rejection of this way of thinking altogether. Understanding is not about the production of 'correct information and scientific knowledge', it is 'a complicated process'. And it is only through this unending activity of thinking that we can 'come to terms with and reconcile ourselves to reality'. This, Arendt councils, is how we make a home in the world.[12]

In a letter to Roger Errera from the summer of 1967 Arendt writes, 'It is, of course, always nice to be praised. But this is really not the point, it's ever so much nicer to be understood.'[13] Perhaps, we might ask, has Hannah Arendt been understood?

In recent years, many people have turned to the work of Hannah Arendt to try to understand the political crises faced today – the decline of liberal democracy, the spread of fake news, the rise of the social sphere, the triumph of technology, the loss of the private realm and the experience of mass loneliness, to name a few. What is it about Arendt's writing that resonates with so many today? Why do we keep turning to her to understand the political conditions of the twenty-first century?

I wager it is because Arendt felt free to look to the past not for analogies, but for those gems, rich and strange, that might help us understand our most recent experiences through a new lens. Like all great political thinkers she was concerned with the problems of her day – the phenomenal appearance of totalitarianism, the politics of revolution, the loss of faith in government, the need for participatory democracy, the decline of culture, the problem of evil.

These questions were not new, but they present themselves to each generation in a new way that requires understanding.

There is also a radical openness in Arendt's writing that invites interpretation and play. Arendt was a poetic thinker. Some have called her an 'and' thinker.[14] In the words of her friend, the political scientist Hans Morgenthau, 'her mind worked in a way not dissimilar to the poetic mind, which creates affinities, which discovers relationships that appear obvious once they are formulated but that nobody had thought of before the poet formulated them.' Arendt knew that meaning was malleable, and that it had to be crafted through storytelling. She wanted to find a new language in order to give voice to a new century of political phenomenon, and she did this by freeing herself from tradition in order to draw together philosophy, theology, political theory, literature and poetry in new constellations.

Arendt was not a superstitious woman. She placed no great weight in oracles or soothsayers. She did not even believe in the myth of progress. Her business was the here-and-now, the everyday lives of ordinary people. Instead of organizing our lives and politics around some notion of a future that can always be better, she thought we should embrace the good.

Arendt was demanding, unapologetic and opinionated. She was not a feminist, a Marxist, a liberal, a conservative, Democrat or Republican. She loved the world and accepted what she understood to be the fundamental elements of the human condition: we do not exist alone, we are all different from one another, we appear, and we will disappear. In between we exist in a space of becoming and we have to care for the earth and build the world in common.

Arendt's love of the world demands that we embrace the human condition. It also demands that we mortals find a way to see the world with all its suffering and love it anyway. This is no easy commandment. Plato dictated that it was better to suffer harm than do harm. Kant gave us the categorical imperative that commanded we will our actions according to the good of all men, arguing the only good is a good will. But when the chips were down, the professional thinkers failed, the nation-state failed and philosophy failed to fight the tide of fascism. So, Arendt broke with tradition. She was fond of quoting the French poet and resistance fighter René Char, who said: 'Our inheritance was left to us by no testament.'

Arendt's work has now become a part of our inheritance, something that we can look to in order to help us in the work of understanding, but she would have protested the use of her work today as an analogy for our present political crises. In an interview shortly before her death, she said, 'To look to the past in order to find analogies by which to solve our present problems is, in my opinion, a mythological error.' What Arendt has to teach us is how to think – how to stop and consider our actions in light of our most recent experiences, fears and desires. Our world today is not the world of the early and mid-twentieth century: it has been radically reshaped by the Cold War, the War on Terror and the rise of digital technology. Arendt shows us how to think the world anew, how to free ourselves from the tradition of Western political thought, how to hold ourselves accountable for our actions, how to think critically without succumbing to ideology. Only when we do this, she says, will we be able to love the world.

In her essay 'Heidegger at 80' Arendt writes, 'Every thinker, if he lives long enough, must strive to unravel what appear as the results of his thoughts, and he does this by rethinking them.' This is not the first biography to be written about Hannah Arendt, nor will it be the last, and I stand with Arendt in imagining how I might have approached it differently. When Elisabeth Young-Bruehl published the first biography of Arendt, *Hannah Arendt: For the Love of the World*, in 1982, she introduced the world to the private life Arendt had kept hidden from the public eye. It is not clear that Arendt ever expected her poems, journals and love letters to be made public knowledge, but she bequeathed them to us in her departure. (Given her work on Rahel Varnhagen's letters and correspondence, it is easy to think she imagined others discovering her papers and finding friendship in them as she had done with Rahel.) Young-Bruehl's biography was modelled on John Peter Nettl's 1966 biography *Rosa Luxemburg*. It is a momentous feat. This biography is of a different sort. It is less comprehensive and more focused. Its aim is to introduce newcomers to the life and work of Hannah Arendt, while filling in some biographical details that have been left out of previous accounts. My hope has been to offer readers a portrait of a woman who was incredibly vivacious, and to illustrate how she was as engaged in the life of action as she was in the life of the mind.

Arendt's passion for understanding and hunger for life are just as important as her ability to engage in self-reflective critical thinking. I do not think the two can be untied, because one must really love the world in order to care for it as deeply as she did. In the darkest hour of her life, when she was in an internment camp with no sense of the future, contemplating suicide, she decided that she loved life too much to give it up. She decided to live, and found laughter in doing so. I hope that her courage in the face of such dark times inspires us to have the courage we need to fight the darkness we face today in this 'none too beautiful world of ours.'[15]

1

Inner Awakening

'Johanna Arendt was born in Linden, Hannover, Germany on 14
October 1906 at a quarter past nine on a Sunday evening.' These
words inscribed by her mother, Martha Cohn, in her *Kinderbuch*
mark the appearance of Hannah Arendt into the world. Martha's
labour lasted 22 hours; Johanna weighed 3,695 grams (8.14 lb).

Hannah Arendt was born at the beginning of the twentieth
century amidst vast social and political transformation: a century
she would later say was defined by 'an uninterrupted chain of wars
and revolutions'.[1] She was the first and only child of Martha and
Paul Arendt. Paul was an electrical engineer, well read in the Greek
and Roman classics; Martha had studied French and music with
a private tutor before travelling abroad. Unlike their parents and
grandparents who had emigrated from Russia, Martha and Paul
were considerably more left-leaning in their politics and religiously
secular.

From the moment Hannah Arendt drew her first breath, her
mother monitored her growth, recording her development in a
book she titled *Unser Kind* (Our Child). The 71 pages dating from
1906 to 1917 contain longform notes that catalogue Hannah's
evolution into personhood: 'The temperament is quiet but alert.
We thought we detected sound perceptions as early as the fourth
week; sight perceptions, aside from general reactions to light, in
the seventh week. We saw the first smile in the sixth week, and
observed a general inner awakening.'[2]

Familiar with the writings of Johann Wolfgang von Goethe and Wilhelm von Humboldt on educational philosophy, Martha wanted to make sure Hannah received a proper upbringing. This distinctly German notion of a *Bildung*, or education, as a form of socialization and self-cultivation, was instilled in all good middle-class citizens. In the 1790s *Bildung* had become a secular social ideal, corresponding to the experiences of the bourgeoisie and aristocracy, offering a philosophy of education for individual success while demanding a reconsideration of social relations. It was not only up to parents to ensure that their children succeeded, it was the task of society to facilitate this process as well. Value was placed on guaranteeing individual freedom, autonomy and self-harmony in order to perfect inner and outer refinement.[3]

But Arendt's sense of inner harmony was challenged early on. At the age of three, her family moved from Hannover to Königsberg, the capital of East Prussia, seeking treatment for her father's syphilis. Paul Arendt had contracted the disease in his youth before he married Martha, and they thought it was in remission when they decided to conceive a child, but by the time Hannah was born he was already in steady decline. After a couple of years he was forced to give up his job as an engineer, and by the summer of 1911 he was placed in a psychiatric hospital, suffering from dementia and paralysis caused by advanced syphilis. Hannah was taken to see him until he could no longer recognize her. She was seven when he died.

After the funeral Martha reflected on Hannah's response to her father's illness and death:

Difficult and sad years lie behind us. The child experiences all of the terrible changes her father suffers from the illness. She is good and patient with him, spent the entire summer of 1911 playing cards with him, doesn't let me say a harsh word about him, but sometimes wishes he wasn't here anymore.

Königsberg, capital of East Prussia, 1900.

She prays for him in the mornings and evenings, without having been taught . . . Paul died in October. She takes that this is something sad for me. She herself is not affected by it. To comfort me she says, 'Remember mom, this happens to a lot of women'. She attended the funeral and cried, 'because the singing was so beautiful'. Otherwise she feels satisfied so many people are paying attention to her. Otherwise, she is a sunny, cheerful child with a good and warm heart.[4]

The experience of losing her father did not diminish Hannah Arendt's inherent wonder at being in the world. From an early age she possessed a combination of shyness, independence and curiosity, coupled with a strong imagination and love of storytelling. Martha records how her daughter's days in kindergarten gave her a variety of ideas for playing at home, re-enacting her lessons from school. She wrote: 'She is always the teacher.'[5]

Hannah was enrolled in kindergarten at the age of four and was required to attend Christian Sunday School like most German

Paul Arendt.

children, regardless of their religious background. Martha was
not observant, but she insisted on sending Hannah to synagogue
with Paul's father Max and his second wife Klara, so she might
have some religious education. Hannah became a student of
Rabbi Vogelstein, seeing him several times a week for religious
instruction. It did not take her long to develop a crush on the rabbi,
and she liked to tell her friends that she intended on marrying him

when she grew up. But her mother warned her that if she did marry the rabbi, she'd have to give up eating pork, to which she replied: 'Well, then, I'll marry a Rabbi with pork.' Hannah did not remain the student for long: soon she was instructing Rabbi Vogelstein that all prayers should be offered to Christ,[6] and not long after that she announced she did not believe in God (though this pronouncement would not stick throughout her life). Religion was something to be understood, not believed. And while she would go on to study theology, this was her first and only taste of religious life.

Hannah's lack of faith, however, did not signal an absence of Jewish identity. Her parents never talked about being Jewish, but she grew up knowing she 'was different'. And it was this difference that would define the terms of her life as a German Jewish woman

Hannah Arendt with her father, Paul.

in the twentieth century. Reflecting on her childhood in a 1964 interview with Günter Gaus, Arendt recounts how she became aware of her Jewish identity:

> The word 'Jew' never came up when I was a small child. I first encountered it through anti-Semitic remarks – they are not worth repeating – from children on the street. After that I was, so to speak, 'enlightened' . . . It wasn't a shock for me at all. I thought to myself: That is how it is. Did I have the feeling that I was something special? Yes. But I could no longer unravel that for you today . . . Objectively, I am of the opinion that it was related to being Jewish. For example, as a child – a somewhat older child then – I knew that I looked Jewish. I looked different from other children. I was very conscious of that. But not in a way that made me feel inferior, that was just how it was . . . You see, all Jewish children encountered anti-Semitism. And the souls of many children were poisoned by it. The difference with me lay in the fact that my mother always insisted that I not humble myself. One must defend oneself![7]

There was a large Jewish population in Königsberg in the early twentieth century. Martha Cohn's father, Jacob Cohn, had fled Russia in 1852 to escape Tsar Nicholas I, whose reign was marked by the oppression of religious minorities. He proclaimed that the Jewish people were a harmful, alien group and adopted policies to systematically destroy Jewish culture through the assimilation of Jewish people. He required compulsory military service for all men, and the seizure of Jewish children from their mothers so that they could be educated within the Christian religion. Jacob Cohn left with his family and founded a tea import firm in Königsberg. Within a few years it developed into a successful business that was able to sustain the family. Jacob died in 1906, the same year that Hannah was born.

The Arendts had been in Königsberg since the eighteenth century and were a well-established and respected family. Max Arendt was chairman of the city council assembly and the liberal Jewish community organization.[8] When Paul and Martha married, they moved into a large house in the Hufen district on Tiergartenstrasse, which came to be known as 'little Moscow'. And even though the Jewish Question was being discussed in Königsberg at the time, it was not talked about in the Arendt home. Her family, like many émigré Jewish families, had assimilated to German life, but when Arendt told her mother what the other schoolchildren had said, Martha instructed her that if she was attacked as a Jew, she had to defend herself as a Jew. Her Jewish identity was not a question or a choice; she was Jewish.

Only a year after her father's death, Hannah's life was disrupted again when the First World War began. After the assassination of Archduke Franz Ferdinand and his wife Sophie on 28 June 1914 in Sarajevo, Austria declared war on Serbia, provoking the Russians to declare war on Austria. As an ally of Austria, Germany entered the war, but instead of going to the Eastern Front, they moved through Belgium to stop the French, which caused the United Kingdom to enter the war. Large red posters announced the declaration of war in Königsberg and called for mobilization; the barracks were flooded with volunteers. Arendt's school class was taken to entertain soldiers as they waited for deployment. Being so close to Russia, East Prussia was a dangerous region to be in, especially for Russian Jews such as Arendt's family. As Russian troops advanced towards Königsberg, tens of thousands of people escaped to occupied territories, including Martha and Hannah. For several weeks they lived in Berlin with Martha's sister Margarete, who was married with three children of her own. Martha described the time in her *Kinderbuch*:

> Terrible days full of excitement, knowing the Russians are
> near Königsberg. On 23 August we fled to Berlin. Hannah
> is enrolled in a Lyzeum in Charlottenburg, where she
> gets along well despite the more advanced classes.
> She finds a lot of love and pampering here with relatives
> and friends. Though there is a strong desire in her for
> home and to return to Königsberg. After a ten-week
> stay, we drive back to the now liberated province.

The German troops had launched a counter-offensive in East Prussia, forcing the Russians to turn back, making it safe for Martha and Hannah to return to Königsberg. Despite the flurry of war activity, Hannah's life mostly returned to normal, but the economic depression facing Germany had impacted the family's finances.[9] After Paul's death, Martha was left with her inheritance and the legacy of the Cohn business to provide for her and Hannah. By the end of the war, with a flailing economy, her resources were dwindling rapidly, and to supplement their income Martha rented a room in their house to a young Jewish student.

The conditions of exile and new home life did not suit Hannah's temperament. In an entry marked January 1914, Martha records Hannah's chronic illnesses, which often corresponded to trips she took. She suffered from a series of nosebleeds, headaches, sore throats, fevers, flu, measles, whooping cough and a case of diphtheria, which the doctor could not confirm. When she was well enough she took piano lessons and learned how to swim, even though, as Martha notes, she didn't have much ability for music or swimming.

During these years Hannah's relationship with her mother changed. The fluctuating social and political circumstances caused her to retreat inward, and her inclination towards always being the teacher became even stronger. She took great pleasure in reading Homer and learning Greek, but she wanted to do it on her own

Hannah, age eight, with her mother, Martha.

terms, not at the instruction of another. In Martha's penultimate *Kinderbuch* entry, she describes her daughter as 'difficult' and 'opaque', and adds that she 'is a very good student, has ambition to be better than the others . . . she learned Latin with her book according to her school's curriculum so well, she wrote the best exam when she returned to school'. Hannah was flourishing intellectually, but the difficult days of her childhood were not over.

On 9 November 1918, during the final days of the war, Kaiser Wilhelm II was forced to abdicate his throne and go into exile, ending the empire and heralding the birth of a new German republic. Two days later on 11 November Germany signed an armistice agreement with the Allies ending the war. The news shocked Germans who thought they were winning. Anger mounted, setting the groundwork for the November Revolution. Although Martha did not support Rosa Luxemburg in the debates with Eduard Bernstein about reform or revolution, she was enthusiastic about the Spartacist uprisings and saw them as a historic moment in German politics. Martha was a lifelong social democrat, and a member of the Communist Party. Other social democrats would often gather at her house to spend long hours around the table in heated debate. Martha introduced Hannah to the ideas of Rosa Luxemburg and took her to see Luxemburg speak at a general strike rally.

Arendt was only thirteen when Rosa Luxemburg and Karl Liebknecht were murdered by the Freikorps in January 1919, but the early imprint of Luxemburg's philosophy and her mother's political activism remained with her. Luxemburg would become an important thinker for Arendt's work on political economy and imperialism in *The Origins of Totalitarianism*, and expropriation in *The Human Condition*. In Luxemburg, Arendt found an independent, passionate woman with whom she could identify, someone who was committed to freedom and participation in public life.

Hannah Arendt as a young girl in Königsberg.

It would take a number of years, though, before Hannah Arendt turned to the world of politics. If the experiences of the Second World War caused her to focus on the public realm, the disruptions caused by the Great War and economic crises in Germany caused her to turn to the life of the mind, towards the world of poetry, philosophy and literature. During the revolutionary years she remained indoors, entrenched in her father's library, reading and memorizing Friedrich Schiller, Goethe, Friedrich Hölderlin and Homer, while exploring philosophy, devouring Karl Jaspers's *Psychology of Worldviews* (1919) and Immanuel Kant's *The Critique of Pure Reason* (1781).

Hannah in her father's library.

In 1964, when Günter Gaus asked her why she chose to study philosophy, theology and Greek, Arendt responded by saying, 'I can only say that I always knew I would study philosophy. Ever since I was fourteen years old.' 'Why?' Gaus presses. Arendt responds: 'I read Kant. You can ask, Why did you read Kant? For me the question was somehow: I can either study philosophy or I can drown myself, so to speak.'

Arendt assures Gaus that she chose to study philosophy, not because she didn't love life, but because she had a 'need to understand'. Her lifelong need to understand was present from the moment she stepped into her father's library: 'You see, all the books were in the library at home; one simply took them from the shelves.'[10] The works Arendt encountered in her youth left a lasting impression, and were formative for shaping the way she thought about Germany after the war. Despite everything, it would be the language of German poetry and philosophy that remained.

In February 1920 Martha married Martin Beerwald, a 46-year-old widowed businessman who was raising two daughters on his own. Martha had known him for some time, and Hannah knew his daughters Eva and Clara, who were nineteen and twenty, from a school project during the war years. After the wedding Martha and Hannah moved in with Martin and his daughters on Busoltstrasse, two streets down from Tiergartenstrasse where Hannah had grown up. Despite the unification of their families, Hannah refused to submit to the authority of her new stepfather. Unlike her stepsisters, who were quiet, demure and plain looking, Hannah was opinionated, rebellious and charming. She made no efforts to become a part of her new family and continued to refuse to attend school on a regular schedule. Elisabeth Young-Bruehl writes, 'Hannah Arendt rose very slowly in the mornings and required several cups of coffee before she could approach sociability.'[11] As with school, Arendt attended family functions rarely, and only

Hannah and her stepsisters, Eva and Clara Beerwald, *c.* 1922.

when she wanted. Around the same time she met Ernst Grumach, an older student who would be responsible for two of the most important relationships of her life: Anne Mendelssohn and Martin Heidegger. Grumach invited Arendt to join a study group he had formed to read Greek and discuss literature and philosophy, and it was in this circle that she learned first about Anne, and then Heidegger.

Anne was a descendant of the great German Jewish philosopher Moses Mendelssohn, who was known as the father of the Jewish Enlightenment, and his grandson Felix Mendelssohn, the

Ernst Grumach, 1920.

composer and pianist. Anne and Hannah's lifelong friendship began in an act of rebellion. Martha had forbidden Hannah from spending time with Anne, because her father, a well-known doctor, had a reputation for salaciousness. He had been accused of sexual harassment by one of his female patients and was serving out a two-year prison sentence. But Hannah did not obey. One night she snuck out of the house after everyone had gone to sleep and took a train to Stolp, a town southwest of Königsberg, where Anne lived. She arrived in the middle of the night and woke up the entire household by throwing stones at the windows. Realizing Arendt was going to be friends with Anne whether she liked it or not, from then on Martha accepted the friendship and Anne was welcome in their home.[12]

Arendt's rebellions continued until she was expelled from school. One day she felt offended by her teacher and organized her schoolmates in a boycott of his classes. Her mother tried to reason with the principal to let her stay in school, but after so many disruptions and missed classes, there was no hope. So Martha arranged for Arendt to finish her schooling at the University of Berlin. At fifteen she moved into a student boarding house and attended classes in Greek, Latin and philosophy. Arendt studied with Romano Guardini, whose open-minded approach to theology, which weaved together poetry and philosophy, inflamed her desire for understanding. She passed the Abitur exams necessary to attend university in Germany with ease, and enjoyed the cultural heyday of the Weimar Republic, removed from the turmoil of German politics.

But Germany was suffering. The Treaty of Versailles was seen as a betrayal by the citizens, inflation was astronomical, the economy was destroyed, and culturally the country was torn between the progressivism of the Weimar Republic and the longing for the front felt by soldiers who had fought in and lost the First World War. Amidst these soldiers was Adolf Hitler, who on 8–9 November

1923 attempted a coup, known as the Beer Hall Putsch, on behalf of the National Socialist Party. Hitler was sentenced to five years in prison for the failed coup and used the time to begin writing his confessions, *Mein Kampf*, which became the manifesto for National Socialism. At the same time, rumours had begun to swirl about a young professor in Marburg who had studied with the great phenomenologist philosopher Edmund Husserl. Ernst Grumach had already attended the first seminars of Martin Heidegger, and he reported back to Hannah Arendt with enthusiasm that the rumours were true: thinking had come to life. He urged her to follow.

2

Shadows

Hannah Arendt arrived at the University of Marburg in the autumn of 1924 shortly before her eighteenth birthday to study with Martin Heidegger.

The German philosopher Karl Löwith referred to Heidegger as 'the little magician from Messkirch' and described his teaching style as 'witchcraft'. Hans-Georg Gadamer, who became known for his work on hermeneutics, called him 'a visionary'. Heidegger was short and handsome with dark hair and a wiry moustache. He dressed in traditional village garb and had a reputation for being charismatic. Students travelled from far away to listen to him lecture, because when he talked about Plato and Aristotle they came to life.

When Arendt appeared in his classroom, Heidegger was 36, married with two sons, and just beginning to work on his masterpiece, *Being and Time*. During her first semester at Marburg, she took Heidegger's lecture course on 'Basic Concepts of Aristotelian Philosophy', and his smaller, seminar-style class on Plato's *Sophist*. The question that drove Heidegger's courses on Plato and Aristotle was: What is the ontological ground of Being? Heidegger was attempting to escape the knot of Western philosophy born from Plato and Aristotle in order to think Being anew.

In *Being and Time* he tried to unearth a new language to address these questions of phenomenology. Heidegger wanted to understand the pre-theoretical conditions for thinking. So, he dug up the tradition of Western philosophy to lay down a 'vast network of thought-paths' and 'trail-marks' in order to open up new dimensions of thought. In a short poem from 1951, Hannah Arendt borrows from Heidegger's language to describe this conception of thinking:

The thoughts come to me,
I am no longer strange to them.
I grow into their dwelling
like a ploughed field.[1]

Born on 26 September 1889 in Messkirch, Baden-Württemberg, to a Catholic family, Heidegger spent the majority of his early years preparing for the priesthood. In 1903 the Church sent him to Konstanz to attend high school, and in 1906 he moved to Freiburg to continue his studies. In the winter semester of 1909 Heidegger entered the Collegium Borromaeum theological seminary. He studied Church history alongside philosophy and biblical exegesis. One of his teachers, Carl Braig, took a particular interest in him and was impressed 'by the incisiveness of his thoughts'.

Braig introduced Heidegger to tensions between ontology and speculative theology, and pointed him towards Aristotle.[2] At the same time, Heidegger began reading Edmund Husserl, moving closer to philosophy and further away from theology. When he read Franz Brentano's 1862 dissertation *On the Manifold Meaning of Being According to Aristotle*, he knew he wanted to pursue the question of thinking. Heidegger left the seminary and enrolled in the philosophy department, where he studied with Heinrich Rickert from 1911 to 1914, before leaving to work with Husserl at the University of Freiburg. Heidegger would later say it was Brentano's book that set him down the path of searching for the meaning of Being.

Martin Heidegger in his library, 1920s.

Despite Hannah Arendt's naturally shy demeanour, she couldn't help but stand out in Marburg, and as much as she delighted in studying alone, she also enjoyed the attention she received from others. In Gadamer's memoir he recalled her during this time as 'the striking girl who always wears a green dress'.[3] She lived in an attic apartment near the university with a pet mouse. The mouse was already in residence when Arendt arrived, but she befriended the lonely creature and entertained her friends when they came to visit by luring him out of his hole with cheese. Arendt's childlike playfulness was one of the many traits that attracted Heidegger to her.

The first time they met alone in his office, he was smitten. Heidegger recounts their meeting in a letter dated 21 March 1925, describing how Arendt had entered in a raincoat, with a hat lowered over her 'large eyes', shyly answering his questions.[4] A few days after their meeting, Heidegger wrote to her:

10 February 1925
Dear Miss Arendt!
I must come see you this evening and speak to your heart.
Everything should be simple and clear and pure between us.
Only then will we be worthy of having been allowed to meet.
You are my pupil and I your teacher, but that is only
the occasion for what has happened to us.
I will never be able to call you mine, but from now on
you will belong in my life, and it shall grow with you.[5]

Less than two weeks later, he professed his love. During the first year of their relationship Arendt and Heidegger met in secret, in his office, in the privacy of her attic apartment, going for long walks in the woods. He wrote her letters in boxy Fraktur script, the true German font, and folded them into squares so no writing would be visible from the outside when he slipped them beneath her door.

Heidegger did not keep Arendt's love letters, but Arendt kept his, and so only a few of her missives survive from this time. The relationship itself did not become public knowledge until after her papers were archived and became available to the public in the 1980s. For Arendt, matters of the heart belonged to the private realm, and she kept her relationship with Heidegger a secret. The only person who knew about their romance was her best friend from childhood, Anne Mendelssohn. Not even her stepsister Clara, who had moved to Marburg, was privy to Arendt's private life.

The letters of Arendt that were saved make clear it was a passionate romance that lasted on and off for several years. In a

Hannah Arendt in the 1920s.

letter dated 18 April 1928 Arendt tells Heidegger that she loved him as she did on the first day they met, and that she would lose her right to live if she lost her love for him.[6]

At the heart of Heidegger's work in *Being and Time* is the concept of *Dasein*. *Dasein* refers to what is distinct about human beings and carries a sense of openness to the being of another. For Heidegger, *Dasein* is not the biological individual, or even the person who appears as an 'I' in this world, but is a kind of selfhood that involves ways of being-a-self, which can be classified as authentic or inauthentic. Being-a-self is self-constituting in and through its interpretation of being, primarily through understanding the world as affording it particular possibilities in light of its facticity, or self-understanding. *Dasein* is difficult to translate, but one may hazard 'being-there'.

With Heidegger, Arendt experienced the authenticity and intensity of *Dasein*, but, as she discovered, when the moment of revelation passes, the veil lifts. And despite the intensity of their romance, Arendt was frustrated by Heidegger's remoteness – due to the demands of his work and family life – as her poems from this period reveal:

Why do you give your hand to me
Shy and like a secret?
Do you come from such a faraway land,
Do you not know our wine?

For Heidegger, philosophy would always come before the women in his life; he needed to be alone in his hut in the woods in Todtnauberg to work out his ideas and write. His wife, Elfriede Petri, whom he had married in 1917 during the First World War, understood this, but Arendt could not. She called the distance between them 'the gap', and it was unbridgeable.

The following summer, in 1925, Hannah Arendt returned home to Königsberg when the semester ended and wrote a self-portrait,

Shadows. *Shadows* is sketched with philosophical language and hues of German Romanticism. The mood is more melancholy than despairing. One senses a kind of hopefulness for a future in her searching lines. Arendt felt alienated from herself by her own sense of wonder, what she called her *Absonderlichkeit*, her strangeness. From her remoteness as a child to her expulsion from her gymnasium and university days in Marburg, Arendt's sense of difference never disappeared, it just changed as she grew older. In a poem written around the same time as *Shadows*, titled 'Absorbed in Oneself', she writes:

When I consider my hand
– Foreign thing related to me –
I stand in no country,
I am not settled in the here and now
I am not settled on anything.

One has a sense when reading Arendt's *Shadows* that she is caught between girlhood and womanhood. Writing in the third person, Arendt frets that she is destined to live her life in 'idle experiments and curiosity without rights or foundations'. She experiences a kind of rootlessness, which confers a great sense of freedom, but also an awareness of the need to ground oneself. She writes, 'Her independence and idiosyncrasy were actually based in a true passion she had conceived for anything odd. Thus, she was used to seeing something noteworthy even in what was apparently the most natural and banal.'[7] Arendt comes back to her own inherent wonder and desire for understanding at the core of her being. She concludes by reflecting on the inevitability of disappearing from the world.

This feeling of melancholy would remain with Arendt throughout her life, but it never diminished her desire for living. Her melancholy is akin to how Aristotle thought about melancholy as a humour, endowing its possessor with a kind of genius and gift for contemplative thinking.

When Arendt finished writing her *Shadows*, she sent one copy to Heidegger, signed 'Königsberg i/PR., April 1925, Geschenk für M.H.' (Gift for M.H.), and bound another with a simple black cover to keep for herself.[8]

After her summer at home, it became clear that her relationship with Heidegger was untenable. She made plans to leave Marburg the following spring, to spend a semester studying in Freiburg with Edmund Husserl before going on to write her dissertation at the University of Heidelberg with Karl Jaspers.

But when Arendt left for Freiburg to study with Husserl, their goodbye was not final. Heidegger kept track of her work at the University of Heidelberg and would ask Karl Jaspers about her progress. Heidegger requested to meet with Arendt in Heidelberg in 1927, the same year in which he published *Being and Time*, but she told him she did not have the time. She had read the manuscript before it was published, and it seems from their correspondence that he sent her extracts from it before it was completed, and asked her for samples of her writing in exchange. In several letters to Arendt Heidegger talks about how his longing for her gave him the energy to write *Being and Time*, but it was precisely his diversion of affection from Arendt towards his work that caused the gap between them to grow.

Heidegger's last letter to Arendt from this period is marked 'Winter 1932/33'. From the letter we can discern that Arendt had written to him about his participation in Nazi activities. Heidegger responds defensively, chronicling his relationships with all of the Jewish people he knew and Jewish students he had mentored.[9] But a few months later, on 21 April 1933, Heidegger was elected as Rector of the University of Freiburg and signed an order to dismiss all faculty not of 'Aryan Descent', including his own mentor Edmund Husserl. On 3 May 1933 he formally joined the National Socialist

Democratic Party, and on 27 May he delivered the inaugural rectoral address on 'The Self-assertion of the German University', which was a statement of support for Hitler. The following November he delivered another address titled 'Declaration of Support for Adolf Hitler and the National Socialist State'.

On 23 April 1934, just a year after his election, he resigned his post as rector. His final address was deemed incompatible with the party line, and was banned by the Nazis. Heidegger had become critical of the regime in his courses, and by 1944 he was declared to be the most 'expendable' member of the faculty. The Nazis sent him to the Rhine to dig trenches for the remainder of the war. After the Second World War, Heidegger was banned from teaching by the Allied occupation authorities until 1951, for his participation in Nazi activities.

In her short essay 'Heidegger the Fox' Arendt describes how Heidegger had been blinded by his philosophical thinking. That he had not seen what was happening, because he had set himself a trap in his thinking: 'Nobody knows the nature of traps better than one who sits in a trap his whole life long.'[10] In a letter dated 9 July 1946 to Karl Jaspers, Arendt reflects upon Heidegger's Nazi activities during the war years, arguing that he should be held accountable for his actions. She tells Jaspers that he should have resigned the moment he was asked to sign the letter dismissing all faculty (including Husserl) who were not of Aryan descent. She writes, 'because I know that this letter and this signature almost killed him, I can't but regard Heidegger as a potential murderer.'[11] Arendt didn't speak to Heidegger for seventeen years.[12]

Arendt never publicly addressed her relationship with Heidegger. She did not often write about romantic love, or the passions. For her they were apolitical. Romantic love turns us away from the world of being together to a world of two. And yet love for Arendt carried with it a great redeeming force.

In her final work, *The Life of the Mind* (1977), she comes to the question of 'willing'. 'Willing' was the most difficult section of the book for her to write, and the one that directly dealt with Heidegger's concept of *Dasein*, love, and the problem of evil. Arendt wanted to understand how it was that one person would do evil, while another would resist. In her analysis of the will she turns to the work of Saint Augustine, who was trying to prove the existence of an omnipotent God. His answer to the problem of evil was that evil is a privation of goodness, caused by the disobedience of human beings. God does not cause evil, but allows it so that humans suffer the consequences of sin. This also allows the possibility for redemption through Jesus Christ. But Arendt was not reading Augustine to prove the existence of God. She did not even believe in the existence of the soul. For her, there is only one world we must face, and it is this one, and in place of divine redemption she turns to a secular concept of love. Will transformed into love has a weight, a gravity which allows it to shape one's character, which allows one to habituate the self into making decisions between different actions. She writes, 'Love is the weight of the soul.'

In love there are three things. There is 'he that loves, and that which is loved, and Love'. Love is not the affection one might feel for a particular object, it is not a form of sentimentality, but rather the 'footprints' and 'sensible things' that leave an impression on the mind. 'In the case of love, the lasting "footprint" that the mind has transformed into an intelligible thing would neither be the one who loves nor his beloved, but the third element, namely, Love itself, the love with which the lovers love each other.' In the transformation of the will into love, what is saved is the will's power. 'There is no greater assertion of something or somebody than to love it, that is, to say, I will that you be – *Amo: Volo ut sis*.' In other words, it is only this love which is capable of bringing about what the mind cannot – lastingness and redemption – and it requires a great release.

3

Love and Saint Augustine

After a semester in Freiburg with Edmund Husserl, Hannah Arendt enrolled at the University of Heidelberg, where she would write her dissertation under the supervision of Karl Jaspers. Jaspers's work introduced Arendt to a new form of philosophical thinking that oriented her towards the world. Unlike Heidegger, who understood thinking to be a solitary enterprise about the self, Jaspers's work on thinking was dialogic and plural.

When Arendt arrived in Heidelberg, Jaspers was just beginning to write his three-part work *Philosophy*, which placed communication at the centre of philosophical activity. His work turned against two of the dominant philosophical schools of the day: Heidegger's phenomenology and neo-Kantianism. Heidelberg, once home to Hegel and the great poets of German Romanticism, remained a vibrant centre for philosophical thought. The sociologist Max Weber and his wife Marianne had established a salon on the other side of the Neckar river, across from the Altstadt and the university. Max Scheler, Georg Simmel, Ernst Bloch and Georg Lukács all crossed paths on the cobblestone streets during these years, but it was Jaspers's relationship with Weber that was decisive for his work. Weber, like Jaspers, took an interdisciplinary approach to his study of philosophy. He wasn't merely interested in the development of abstract ideas, he was curious about the nature of the human condition, and the intersections between social and political thought.

When Jaspers finished his habilitation (a second book to secure a teaching position), he became a practising psychiatrist and taught courses on the ethical and moral dimensions of social psychology. But his work was considered too philosophical to be taken seriously by psychologists. So, nearing forty, Jaspers decided to take a leap from psychology to philosophy and began working on his *Psychology of Worldviews*. When *Psychology* was published in 1919, he applied for a faculty position at the University of Heidelberg and wrote to Heinrich Rickert, a leading philosopher there who had been Heidegger's teacher. Rickert not only turned Jaspers away, he protested his application, arguing that Jaspers was not a real philosopher. Despite Rickert's efforts, Jaspers was hired at the University of Heidelberg as a professor of philosophy in 1922.

For Jaspers, philosophy was oriented around lived experience. As a psychiatrist he was interested in the psychology of scientific knowledge, and as a philosopher he was interested in epistemology. In this way, Jaspers's *Existenzphilosophie* emerged out of the late eighteenth- and early nineteenth-century tradition of German Idealism, and *Selbstbewusstsein*, or self-knowledge. His understanding of philosophy was more expansive than German Idealism permitted, however. This is evidenced most clearly in Jaspers's debates with Rickert, who had also studied with Max Weber. Like Heidegger, Jaspers was interested in questions of Being, but his existentialist approach was fundamentally at odds with Heidegger's understanding of phenomenology. By moving away from Kant and Hegel, Jaspers was able to transform the fundamental questions of metaphysics. For him, the world as it appears is phenomenal, and this phenomenal reality is concerned with categories of understanding, not the accumulation of scientific knowledge that claims certain truth. Jaspers was after what he called authentic knowledge. His question was: How should a person be in the world? And to answer this question, he placed communication, transcendence and freedom at the centre of his work.

Jaspers's lectures were not a transmission of ideas, but rather 'a mode of communication'.[1] Like Socrates speaking to Agathon in Plato's *Symposium*, he believed that wisdom was not something that could flow between two people, like wine from a full bottle into an empty glass. Instead, learning had to come through a process of conversation. He was interested in a language that could remain open to the possibilities of human experience, which required one to be receptive in conversation. His seminars on the German Idealist Friedrich von Schelling, modes of thinking, and thinking processes, were concerned with questions of philosophy's nature. Jaspers's methodology in thinking and teaching had been influenced by Weber's framework for working on ideal types, human behaviour, cultural phenomena and the limitations of such typologies to illuminate why people adopt a particular world-view – or, more plainly put, what moves people to think, act and make certain choices. For Jaspers, answers had to be found in reality looking towards the world, not in the mode of pure philosophical contemplation.

These central elements of Jaspers's philosophy left a lasting impression on Hannah Arendt's work. At the centre of her conception of thinking is conversation, or the 'two-in-one' dialogue one has with oneself. Studying with Jaspers meant that, for Arendt, thinking was no longer confined to a hidden realm. Her dissertation work on the theologian and philosopher Saint Augustine drew together the disciplines of theology and philosophy in order to understand neighbourly love as a secular value for being with others in the world.

During Arendt's time together with Heidegger in Marburg, Heidegger had been reading Augustine's *On Grace and Free Will*. When he later wrote to Arendt, on the subject of her *Shadows*, he quotes from Augustine:

Thank you for your letters – for how you have accepted me into your love – beloved. Do you know that this is the most difficult thing a human is given to endure? For anything else, there are methods, aids, limits and understanding – here alone everything means: to be in one's love = to be forced into one's innermost existence. *Amo means volo, ut sis*, Augustine once said: 'I love you – I want you to be what you are.'

Because of this, Arendt's first biographer, Elisabeth Young-Bruehl, speculated that Arendt's dissertation on *Love and Saint Augustine* was a reflection on the end of her relationship with Heidegger. If this is the case, it is not readily apparent in the text, and only true in the sense that Arendt's work is about neighbourly love, which is worldly, unlike romantic love, which turns one inwards. Other Arendt scholars have found it curious that a young Jewish student studying with the two leading existentialist philosophers of her day would write about a Christian bishop and saint at all. When asked this question many years later, her friend Hans Jonas, whom she had met in Heidegger's seminar in 1925, said, 'such a topic would not have been all that unusual in the German universities of the time'.[2] Jonas himself had come to Heidelberg to write his first book on *Augustine and the Pauline Problem of Freedom* (1930). At the time, Christian philosophers such as Augustine, Blaise Pascal and Søren Kierkegaard were popular thinkers to study, and the problem of Christianity and modernity was a timely topic about which to write.

Arendt's dissertation on *Love and Saint Augustine* established her as an independent thinker, indebted to her teachers and the tradition of German philosophy. In Augustine's conception of neighbourly love, Arendt found a way of being that turned towards the world of lived experience. Through Augustine's distinctions between *amor, cupiditas* and *caritas*, she arrived at her understanding of Amor Mundi – 'love of the world': 'It is through love of the world that man explicitly makes himself at home in the world, and then desirously looks to it alone for his good and evil. Not until then do the world and man grow "worldly".'[3]

With the help of Jaspers, *Love and Saint Augustine* was published by Julius Springer in 1929 and caused an intellectual stir. It was reviewed by some of the major journals of the time, including *Philosophisches Jahrbuch*, *Kantstudien*, *Gnomon* and *Deutsche Literatur-Zeitung*. Many of the reviews were not favourable. They thought that she had ignored Augustine as a theologian. Other commentators complained that she had produced an idiosyncratic reading of *caritas*. Arendt had written a book about Saint Augustine without consulting the literature on Augustine, or reading Augustine scholars, because she was neither reading Saint Augustine as a theologian nor offering a history of early Christian thought. She approached his *Confessions* as a text to be read through an existential lens that could help her think about plurality and neighbourly love as constituent forces for building the world in common. Jaspers's *Existenzphilosophie* had taught her that true being is inseparable from worldliness. Despite her detractors, Arendt received 'full marks for her originality and insight'.

Arendt did not return to her dissertation manuscript until the mid-1950s, but Augustine remained an interlocuter throughout her life. The language of new beginnings, neighbourly love and love of the world appears in *The Origins of Totalitarianism*, *The Human Condition*, *On Revolution*, *Eichmann in Jerusalem*, *Between Past and Future* and *The Life of the Mind*.

In 1953, when she was working on 'Ideology and Terror', which became the final chapter in *Origins*, Arendt turned to Augustine to reflect on new beginnings and offer readers a glimpse of well-measured hope:

But there remains also the truth that every end in history necessarily contains a new beginning; this beginning is the promise, the only 'message' which the end can ever produce. Beginning, before it becomes a historical event, is the supreme capacity of man; politically, it is identical with man's freedom. *Initium ut esset homo creatus est* – 'that a beginning be made man was created' said Augustine. This beginning is guaranteed by each new birth; it is indeed every man.[4]

Every end in history marks a new beginning, the outcome of which cannot be predicted. Arendt published her dissertation in 1929, and carried the paperback copy with her when she was forced into exile in 1933. For a while she thought it was lost after she knocked it into a bathtub in Paris, but fortunately she had sent another copy to Gershom Scholem, the historian and philosopher of Jewish mysticism, which he agreed to return to her.

During Arendt's time in Heidelberg she found an intellectual community and became friends with a group of students whom she had met studying philosophy and psychology. Karl Frankenstein, a professor of psychology at Hebrew University, Erich Neumann, a Jungian psychoanalyst, and the essayist Erwin Loewenson, who wrote about the Expressionist school. In 1927, shortly after ending her relationship with Heidegger, Arendt and Loewenson, who was nearly twenty years her senior, had an affair, which lasted a little less than a year. Their letters written between 1927 and 1928, and after the war, are mostly about their scholarly interests. Despite Arendt's attraction to Loeweson's poetic style, his emotional instability led her to end the relationship.

Soon after she began dating Benno Georg Leopold von Wiese und Kaiserswaldau. He was only three years older than Arendt and had just finished his dissertation on Friedrich Schlegel under the tutorship of Karl Jaspers. Unlike Heidegger and Loewenson, von Wiese was very much a part of the world, and a leading intellectual and social figure in Heidelberg. He had been a student of German Romanticism and studied with Friedrich Gundolf, the leading professor of literature in Germany at the time. Von Wiese took Arendt to Gundolf's lectures and introduced her to the world of

Unidentified woman,
Hugo Friedrich,
Hannah Arendt and
Benno von Wiese
in Heidelberg,
Germany, *c.* 1928.

literary Romanticism. Arendt began attending salons with von Wiese and smoking a metal-stemmed pipe, while formulating her second book, which was to be a critique of German Romanticism. Despite their intellectual rapport, von Wiese decided that Arendt was not the wife he was looking for; he wanted someone more domestic to take care of the home and support his work. After two years of dating, they went their separate ways, but Arendt continued working on the Jewish salon tradition while preparing her habilitation on Rahel Varnhagen.

4

Life of a Jewess

On 29 October 1929 the stock market on Wall Street collapsed. Black Tuesday, as it came to be known, sent the world's financial markets into a nosedive. Germany's economy was particularly vulnerable after the First World War since it was rebuilt on foreign capital, mostly with American loans. Additionally, foreign countries had placed protective tariffs on German goods, which meant repaying the loans was not possible. Faced with mounting debt, Germany began printing more money, which created a state of hyperinflation, rendering the Deutschmark worthless. As the Great Depression hit, the United States sought immediate repayment of their loans to Germany, bringing the economy to its knees. As the German economy ground to a halt, production levels fell and workers were laid off. Inflation continued to rise and the middle classes were quickly depleted. By the winter of 1930 more than 2 million Germans had lost their jobs. By 1933 one in three Germans was unemployed.

Amidst rising unemployment costs and high government expenditures, the people's faith in democracy began to falter. By the spring of 1930 Chancellor Hermann Müller resigned and was replaced by Heinrich Brüning. In July 1930 Brüning cut government spending, wages and unemployment in a bid to fix the economy, but the Reichstag resisted his actions, so Brüning asked President Hindenburg to invoke Article 48 of the German constitution, giving emergency powers to the president to rule by decree. That September the Nazi Party gained 18.3 per cent of the vote, becoming the second largest party in the Reichstag. By the summer of 1932 the National Socialist Party had grown to 450,000 members. Adolf Hitler seized the moment and initiated a massive campaign, running for president against Hindenburg, attacking the Weimar Republic, while pledging to dissolve the parliamentary system. When presidential elections were held in April 1932, Hitler won 36.8 per cent of the vote. Brüning resigned at the end of May and Hindenburg appointed a conservative, Franz von Papen, as his replacement. During the Reichstag elections that July the Nazi Party became the largest party, with 230 seats, but they still did not have a majority. Von Papen called for Reichstag elections in November in a bid to win a majority. Although the Nazi Party lost 34 seats, von Papen was uncertain he could survive a vote of no-confidence. The next month von Papen resigned and Hindenburg appointed General Kurt von Schleicher as Chancellor. Von Schleicher asked Gregor Strasser to be his Vice Chancellor, but Hitler ordered him to decline. And on 30 January 1933 Adolf Hitler was appointed Chancellor of Germany, with von Papen as Vice Chancellor.[1]

During these years Hannah Arendt was working on her habilitation, *Rahel Varnhagen: The Life of a Jewish Woman*. Her childhood friend Anne Mendelssohn had been reading Varnhagen's correspondence, which she happened upon by chance in a bookshop that had gone bankrupt and was forced to sell its stock. Anne had introduced Arendt to Varnhagen's work before she left for Heidelberg, but Arendt didn't take an interest in her until she began working on German Romanticism. When Arendt told Anne about her work, Anne gave her the collection of correspondence.

In Varnhagen, Arendt found her 'closest friend' and 'a woman with a truly passionate nature'. She also found a biographical example of the dangers of romantic individualism, Jewish assimilation and the rise of anti-Semitism in Europe. And, unlike most of her peers, by 1929 Hannah Arendt was already attuned to the political situation unfolding in Germany, in large part because of her work on Varnhagen.

Rahel understood herself to be 'a *schlemihl* and a Jewess', and she spent the better part of her life trying to assimilate into bourgeois society in order to escape her Jewish identity, going so far as to convert to Christianity when she married Karl August Varnhagen von Ense in 1814. Born without the privilege of great beauty, she made her mark conversationally through the salons she hosted. Rahel was an admirer and friend of Goethe and exemplified a new kind of modern, romantic subject that took flight from the world. Her own writing, mostly contained in letters, typifies the heightened self-reflective consciousness of the day.

Arendt wanted to tell Rahel's story as she might have told it herself, abandoning chronology and historicism. There is little material detail in the work. Instead, one meets Rahel's voice and Arendt's judgement. Arendt drew from Rahel's letters, which had been selected and edited by her husband Karl August after her death, and the unpublished materials held in the Prussian State Library. Rahel Varnhagen was the first Jewish woman to establish herself as a leading intellectual and political figure in Germany. Born in Berlin in 1771, Varnhagen came to host one of the most prominent salons in Europe, entertaining the great German Romantic poets and thinkers such as Friedrich Schlegel, Friedrich Schelling, Henrik Steffens, Friedrich Schleiermacher, Wilhelm von Humboldt and Ludwig Tieck. Although she never penned a major work, her correspondence contains more than 6,000 letters.

In Arendt's essay 'Walter Benjamin', she describes Benjamin's style as 'tearing fragments out of their context and arranging them afresh in such a way that they illustrated one another and were able to prove their *raison d'être* in a free-floating state, as it were'. This is how Arendt wrote Rahel, weaving together long series of quotations and exegetical analysis. Using literary montage, dreamscapes and psychological reflection, Arendt's *Rahel* stands out in the body of her work. In 1958 the English novelist Sybille Bedford reviewed the book and said it is 'a relentlessly abstract book – slow, cluttered, static, curiously oppressive; reading it feels like sitting in a hot-house with no watch. One is made to feel the subject, the waiting, distraught woman; one is made aware, almost physically, of her intense femininity, her frustration.'[2] Understanding Arendt's approach to Rahel, one might read this review as a success.

Before Arendt fled Berlin in 1933 she had finished the first eleven chapters of *Rahel Varnhagen*. She completed the last two chapters during the summer of 1938 in exile at the urging of her second husband, Heinrich Blücher, and her friend Walter Benjamin, but she did not revisit the text for publication until after the war.[3] The first title Arendt contemplated for her work on Rahel Varnhagen was 'On the Problem of German-Jewish Assimilation Exemplified in the Life of Rahel Varnhagen'. As with her work on Augustine, Arendt's habilitation was thought lost, but it was saved thanks to Käthe Fürst (the wife of Arendt's cousin, Ernst) who had carried a copy with her to Palestine before the war began. The manuscript was returned to Arendt in 1945.

The poet Hermann Broch said Arendt's *Rahel Varnhagen* was a 'new type of biography', woven together like 'a Gobelin tapestry'. He thought Arendt's account was a kind of amorous record, outlining the various love affairs Rahel had entertained. He said it was a kind of 'abstract pornography'. When Karl Jaspers read the book for the first time in 1952, he responded reticently to the text, encouraging her to 'rework the whole book at such a time as inclination and circumstances' permit. He was worried that the work did not reflect Arendt's intellectual talents.[4] Arendt was not surprised by Jaspers's response. She admits that it was a mottled procedure, interrupted by war. When she came back to finish it in exile, she wrote from the perspective of a Zionist critique of assimilation, which she had since distanced herself from. She tells Jaspers,

> that critique was as politically naïve as what it was criticizing. Personally, the book is alien to me in many ways, and perhaps that's why I feel it as particularly alien to me now, especially in its tone, in its mode of reflection, but not in the Jewish experience, which I made my own with no little difficulty.[5]

The dense prose style of *Rahel Varnhagen* makes Arendt's critique of German Romanticism and the Enlightenment easy to miss. Her indictment of Rahel's introspection and desire for escape is a critique of the kind of individualism produced by Romanticism.

Whereas Arendt's work on Saint Augustine's *Confessions* gave her a framework for thinking about what it means to turn towards the world, Rahel Varnhagen's letters gave Arendt a framework for thinking about the kind of individualism that turned one away from the world. And in this style of heightened individualism, which favoured social assimilation, Arendt saw the early seeds of anti-Semitism that were spreading across Germany.

At the centre of Arendt's biography are the words Rahel uttered on her deathbed: 'The things which all my life seemed to me the greatest shame, which was the misery and misfortune of my life – having been born a Jewess – this I should on no account now wish to have missed.' Rahel's struggle to acknowledge her Jewish identity illustrated the extent to which assimilation had erased the traditions of Jewish people in Germany. In her analysis, Arendt drew a distinction between the parvenu, or upstart, the pariah, who is cast from society for being different, and the conscious pariah, who takes hold of their otherness and carries it proudly through the world. For Arendt, conscious pariahdom was the only option, and it was a way to resist the tide of assimilation.

In January 1929 Hannah Arendt met Günther Anders (Stern) at a New Year's masquerade ball in Berlin at the Museum of Ethnology. Anders was a dashing, swarthy gentleman; Arendt was dressed as a harem girl in Arabian garb. The Bal de Paris was an event for a Marxist group Anders belonged to, and they were trying to raise money to begin a magazine. They had encountered one another four years earlier in Martin Heidegger's seminar on 'The Concept of Time,' but did not really become aquainted then. Heidegger's wife did not like Anders because he was Jewish, and Heidegger had complained about Anders in his letters decrying him as 'just one of the worst'.[6] Anders had written a letter to Heidegger admitting that he had published a paper in which he couldn't distinguish Heidegger's ideas from his own, and Heidegger was convinced Anders was grifting off his work.

In a small book titled *The Cherry Battle*, which Anders wrote after Arendt's death, he recounts the beginning of their relationship: 'I won Hannah at a ball while dancing; I remarked that love is the act in which one transforms an a posteriori – the other person one has encountered by coincidence – into the a priori of one's own life. Of course this beautiful formula was not confirmed.'[7] After a month of dating, Arendt and Anders moved in together, and the following September they were married in a small civil ceremony.

When friends later asked Arendt what drew her to Anders, she told them he was a 'kind and gentle man', and recounted a story about falling ill with a sore throat soon after they met. Anders 'appeared with a basket of lemons and his good humour'. In *The Cherry Battle* Anders describes Arendt during the time as being 'profound, cheeky, cheerful, domineering, melancholic, and always ready to dance'.[8] It also helped that Arendt's mother was quite fond of Anders. He was a socialist from a well-established German-Jewish family and Martha enjoyed his company.[9] His parents, William and Clara Stern, were renowned child psychologists

Hannah Arendt and Günther Anders (Stern), *c.* 1929.

who had published a well-known book on parenting titled *The Psychology of Early Childhood up to the Sixth Year* (1914; an English edition was published in 1924). The work drew heavily on the observational diaries Clara Stern kept during the first six years of her children's lives. Clara and William Stern were also central to the development of the Intelligence Quotient (IQ).

Like Arendt, Anders had a typical middle-class childhood that was uprooted by the onset of the First World War. During the war years he was, along with thousands of other students, involved in organizing aid in the German war effort on the Western Front, serving in a paramilitary organization that harvested crops for the army in France. After completing his high-school education, he studied in Hamburg with the neo-Kantian philosopher Ernst Cassirer and the art historian Erwin Panofsky. After a brief stretch in Munich with Heinrich Wölfflin, he went to Berlin to study with the psychologists Eduard Spranger, Wolfgang Köhler and Max Wertheimer, before finally going to the University of Freiburg to write his dissertation under the direction of Edmund Husserl. By the time he met Arendt in Heidegger's seminar in 1926, he was working on his habilitation, while serving as an assistant to Max Scheler.[10]

Arendt and Anders had a similar philosophical training, having studied with Husserl, Heidegger and Jaspers, and their shared history allowed for an easy relationship. Anders helped Arendt revise her dissertation for publication, and Arendt edited his writing; together they co-authored an article on Rainer Maria Rilke's *Duino Elegies*.

Günther Stern took the name Anders at the beginning of his publishing career. There are two accounts of why he chose to change his last name. One comes from Elisabeth Young-Bruehl, the other from Hans Jonas. According to Young-Bruehl, when Anders went to work with the poet and playwright Bertolt Brecht on the transcript of a radio broadcast, Brecht was so impressed with Stern's work he helped him find a position through his friend

Herbert Ihering, who hired him to be a staff reporter for the *Berlin Börsen-Courier*. Apparently Anders began writing so much, the editor asked him to take a *nom de plume*, so it would appear they had more writers. According to Hans Jonas, however, he changed his name because 'Stern' immediately associated him with his well-known parents: 'Someone had said to him: "You can go by a different [*anderen*] name." To which he responded: "Alright, then I call myself Anders."'[11]

After their wedding in September 1929 Arendt and Anders moved to Frankfurt so that he could work on his habilitation with Paul Tillich at the Institute for Social Research at the University of Frankfurt. Shortly after arriving, Anders presented his proposal to Tillich, Theodor Adorno, Max Horkheimer, Max Wertheimer and Karl Mannheim. It was initially met with favour and Adorno suggested he focus on the philosophy of music. For the next year Arendt and Anders lived in a sexton's cottage near the River Main in Frankfurt and worked on their respective habilitations. But when Anders submitted his work in 1930 it was met with disapproval by Tillich and Adorno. Anders's thesis had been influenced by the work of Martin Heidegger and, with the brewing political situation, Anders was advised to wait until 'the Nazi-hype' had abated.[12]

Arendt blamed Adorno for Anders's failed habilitation. When they first met, she had been put off by his demeanour. Shortly after their arrival Anders suggested they invite him to dinner, to which she responded, 'Der kommt uns nicht ins Haus!' (That one's not coming into our house). The rejection of Anders's habilitation was only confirmation of her distaste. Arendt's animosity towards Adorno was personal and philosophical. She was not fond of the so-called Frankfurt School and their idea of Critical Theory. In Max Horkheimer's essay 'Traditional and Critical Theory', which can be read as a methodological statement for the Institute, he argues the work of Critical Theory aims at transforming society as a whole by examining the underlying social relations that shape the world.

Arendt came from a different tradition of thought. Adorno and Horkheimer rejected the traditions of phenomenology, which laid an ontological foundation for how people experience existence. She was influenced by Aristotle's conception of politics, Immanuel Kant's understanding of reason and judgement, Heidegger's phenomenology, and Jaspers's existentialism. These elements in Arendt's thinking could not be reconciled with Adorno's Marxist economics, Hegelian dialectics and inclination towards social psychology.[13]

Despite Arendt's antipathy towards the Institute for Social Research, she formed a personal friendship with Paul Tillich that would continue in the United States, and maintained a professional relationship with Karl Mannheim while taking his seminars at the Institute. When Mannheim's *Ideology and Utopia* was published in 1929, Arendt reviewed it for *Die Gesellschaft*, one of the leading socialist journals. The editor, Rudolf Hilferding, was friends with Arendt's mother and wanted a critical review of the book because he thought the argument posed a threat to socialism. Arendt's review focused on Mannheim's claims about thinking. She asked: 'how can thought, if it is anchored in a socio-economic situation, be said to ignore the situation? If thinking can ignore the actual situation, then its root must be elsewhere; and that would imply that thought is not simply action's servant.'[14] This argument would come to play an integral part in Arendt's conceptualizing of *The Human Condition* and work on 'Thinking', showing how thinking was an activity in itself that had to be rooted in worldly experience.

After two years working on his failed habilitation, Anders left the Institute for Social Research, and he and Arendt moved back to Berlin. During their time in Frankfurt Arendt had been working on her study of German Romanticism, while working as a freelance journalist for the *Frankfurter Zeitung*. She published a short article on 'Augustine and Protestantism' to mark the fifteen hundredth anniversary of Augustine's death, and wrote a review of Alice Rühle-Gerstel's *Das Frauenproblem der Gegenwart* (The Contemporary Woman's Problem). Later in the United States, during the height of the women's liberation movement, Arendt would write that she swore a 'holy oath' to never touch the question of women's liberation. But in her review of Rühle-Gerstel's work, she addressed it head on:

> For, although today's women have the same rights legally as men, they are not valued equally by society. Economically, their equality is reflected in the fact that in many cases they work for a considerably lower wage than men. If they were to work on the same pay scale, they would – in keeping with their social value – simply lose their positions of employment ... The average situation of the professional woman is much more complicated. Not only must she accept, despite her legal equality, less remuneration for her work, but also she must continue to do socially and biologically grounded tasks that are incompatible with her new positions. In addition to her profession, she must take care of her household and raise her children. Thus a woman's freedom to make her own living seems to imply either a kind of enslavement in her own home or the dissolution of her family.[15]

Arendt wasn't against socio-economic equality for women, she was against the ideological character of the 'women's movement'. For Arendt, the professional woman was an economic fact, and a political movement could not attend to the particularity and complexity of women's lives. Which is to say, the unequal treatment of women was a feature of society that had to be remedied through broader political change. Arendt's position echoes the argument Rosa Luxemburg made in her 1912 essay 'Women's Suffrage and Class Struggle'. Like Luxemburg, Arendt was unapologetically a woman, but just because one is born a woman, doesn't mean one belongs to a women's movement. For Arendt and Luxemburg, the unequal treatment of women was an economic problem that reflected larger social and political problems that had to be addressed. Attempts to conscript women by virtue of their sex into a political movement was seen as an erasure of difference. The aim should not be to make women equal to men socially, because men and women are fundamentally different from one another; the aim should be to put right the economic inequalities that prevent women from participating in politics, through economic disadvantage. In a 1966 book review of J. P. Nettl's biography of Rosa Luxemburg, Arendt criticizes Nettl's inability to understand Luxemburg's position on the woman question:

> There is another aspect of her personality which Nettl stresses but whose implications he seems not to understand; that she was so 'self-consciously a woman'. This in itself put certain limitations on whatever her ambitions otherwise might have been – for Nettl does not ascribe to her more than what would have been natural in a man with her gifts and opportunities. Her distaste for the women's emancipation movement, to which all other women of her generation and political convictions were irresistibly drawn, was significant; in the face of suffragette equality, she might have been tempted to reply, *Vive la petite différence*. She was an outsider, not only because she was and remained a Polish Jew in a country she disliked and a party she came soon to despise, but also because she was a woman. Mr. Nettl must, of course, be pardoned for his masculine prejudices.[16]

Attuned to the rise of anti-Semitism in Germany, and changing social and political conditions that accompanied the collapse of the Weimar Republic, Arendt began spending time at the Hochschule für Politik in Berlin, where she met Albert Salomon and Sigmund

Kurt Blumenfeld in Königsberg, Prussia, August 1925.

Neumann. Between 1931 and 1933 Arendt also began reading Karl Marx and Leon Trotsky intensely, while spending more time with her friend Kurt Blumenfeld. Blumenfeld and Arendt had long conversations about Zionism while smoking Black Havanas, which Anders hated. He did not approve of Arendt's 'masculine' behaviour. He thought it was unbecoming for her to smoke pipes and cigars with the men, and to be spending so much time with Blumenfeld, whom he saw as a bad influence. As Arendt became more political, her marriage with Anders began to unravel. He did not like her independent behaviour, and she did not like his disapproval.

5

Turn Towards Politics

Between 1929 and 1933 Hannah Arendt ended her relationship with Martin Heidegger, wrote and published her dissertation on *Love and Saint Augustine*, began working on *Rahel Varnhagen*, married and separated from her first husband Günther Anders, and was forced to flee into exile. Unlike many of her friends and acquaintances during these years, Arendt was attuned to the dire political situation developing around her. When she saw the burning of the Reichstag on 27 February 1933, she knew she had to act. Many years later she said: 'From that moment on I felt responsible. That is, I was no longer of the opinion that one can simply be a bystander.'[1]

Adolf Hitler's use of violence, attack on civil liberties and suspension of rights following the Reichstag fire made it clear to Arendt that she had to leave Germany. It also made it clear to her that she had to leave the world of academic philosophy in order to face what was happening politically. The assumption that philosophy was supposed to equip one to act in a moral manner failed when tested by reality. Intellectuals were no better prepared than anyone else to act with courage when confronted with Nazification. *Gleischschaltung*, or political coordination, became the rule. Professors and intellectuals chose to secure their positions instead of resisting.

In her 1946 review essay 'The Image of Hell', published in *Commentary*, Arendt talks about how some academics in Germany tried to justify their capitulation:

If anybody wants a real glance at the physiognomy of the average German professor under Hitler he should read the candid confession of Gerhard Ritter, professor of history at Freiburg, in April, 1946, *Review of Politics*. This anti-Nazi professor kept his real opinions so secret and had so little knowledge of what was going on that he could feel that 'the machinery of the Hitler Reich . . . did not function well.' And he was so involved in the 'deeper life of the intellect,' so busy preventing 'the inevitable damage from becoming too great,' and so convinced of his chances to 'publish . . . independent views on historico-political questions' – although 'there were certain impassable limits to [his] freedom as a teacher' – that the Gestapo, to his own great surprise, decided to use him for propaganda abroad.[2]

Arendt's ironic tone in this passage is important for her understanding of judgement, and is characteristic of her style in her early essays on the Holocaust, and her later work *Eichmann in Jerusalem* (1963). Irony allows for distance and reveals logical absurdity with a sense of humour. Arendt refused to make sense of the incomprehensible; her tone was a way of offering critique through form. To have written in a very serious matter would have been to take very seriously something illogical and horrific by all measures. It was necessary to be able to laugh in the face of those who did evil, because sometimes laughter is all one has to assert their dignity. And when confronted with such evil, Arendt remembered what her mother told her the first time she encountered anti-Semitism: 'If one is attacked as a Jew, one must defend oneself as a Jew. Not as a German, not as a world-citizen, not as an upholder of the Rights of Man, or whatever.'[3] For Arendt the question was clear: 'What can I specifically do as a Jew?' She put down her manuscript on *Rahel Varnhagen*, but not without acknowledging the irony that 1933 marked the hundredth anniversary of Rahel's death.

That March, shortly after the burning of the Reichstag, Günther Anders fled when he learned the Gestapo had confiscated Bertolt Brecht's address book. There was fear among leftists that it would be used to arrest communists throughout the city. As Anders made his way to Paris, Arendt stayed behind in Berlin and turned their apartment on Opitzstrasse, near Breitenbachplatz, into a stop on the underground network to help communists flee. Her mother Martha and niece Else Aron came to help her, providing cover for strangers that arrived and left at all hours of the day. Arendt gave her mother and niece instructions for answering the phone, and Martha used her social network from political organizing to bring news about which leftists groups were being arrested. Legality no longer mattered. The old moral categories of right and wrong could not be counted upon for thinking about how to act under such circumstances. The only way to be a conscientious person was to become an outlaw.

Her friend, the Zionist organizer Kurt Blumenfeld, asked her to collect anti-Semitic statements in newspapers, journals and speeches from the Prussian State Library for the German Zionist Organization. At the time this was an illegal activity the Nazis called 'horror propaganda'. The collection of articles was to be sent to foreign press offices and world leaders, to show how widespread anti-Semitism had become in Germany, and used at the 18th Zionist Congress that summer in Prague. For several weeks Arendt sat in the Prussian State Library sifting through newspaper articles and statements from all kinds of professional clubs and organizations collecting anti-Semitic remarks. And then one afternoon, as she was leaving to meet her mother for lunch, she was arrested. A worker at the library had reported her unusual reading activity to the Gestapo. 'What use does an academic have with so many newspapers?'

The young officer who arrested Arendt took her and her mother to the police station at Alexanderplatz for questioning. On the way Arendt complained that she had only a few cigarettes and asked if they could stop to buy some more. The officer pulled over the car, bought her several packs, and told her how she could smuggle them into her cell. Another officer held Martha and questioned her in a separate room while they searched Arendt's apartment. Martha did not reveal anything to the officers and responded with a mother's instinct: 'No, I do not know what she was doing, but whatever she was doing she was right to be doing it and I would have done the same.'[4]

The only thing the officers could find in Arendt's apartment was a collection of old notebooks, which they brought in to inspect. Over several days they interrogated her about the meaning of the writing in the notebooks, asking her if it was some kind of secret code, while she tried to explain to them that it was Greek. The officers had found a collection of her philosophy notebooks.

Arendt described her arrest in an interview with Günter Gaus as 'very lucky'. She was well aware that many who were arrested were being thrown into cellars, murdered or transported to camps.

I got out after eight days because I made friends with the official who arrested me. He was a charming fellow! He'd been promoted from the criminal police to a political division. He had no idea what to do. What was he supposed to do? He kept saying to me, 'Ordinarily I have someone there in front of me, and I just check the file, and I know what's going on. But what shall I do with you?' . . . Unfortunately, I had to lie to him. I couldn't let the organization be exposed. I told him tall tales, and he kept saying, 'I got you in here. I shall get you out again. Do not get a lawyer! Jews do not have any money now. Save your money!' Meanwhile the organization had gotten me a lawyer. Through members, of course. And I sent this lawyer away. Because the man who arrested me had such an open and decent face. I relied on him and thought that here was a much better chance than with some lawyer who himself was afraid.[5]

Hannah Arendt's German passport photograph, 1933.

The next day Hannah and her mother Martha fled Germany, but not without first saying goodbye to their friends. Arendt, the girl who had cried listening to the beautiful music at her father's funeral, knew there was always light in dark times. The night of her release was, in the words of Anne Mendelssohn, 'the most drunken occasion' of their lives.[6]

When they left on foot the next morning they carried little with them: diplomas, birth, marriage and death certificates, a copy of *Rahel Varnhagen*, and the 24 poems Arendt had written between

1923 and 1926. They made their way towards Prague through the Erzgebirge (Ore Mountains), which were known to the refugees as the 'Green Front'. Leftists had organized a network of border stations there to help people escape. Hannah and Martha were directed to Karlsbad, where a family owned a house with a front door in Germany and back door in Czechoslovakia. They arrived in the afternoon, ate dinner and left through the back door at night.[7]

After a brief stay in Prague, Arendt and Martha left for Geneva to meet up with one of Martha's friends, Martha Mundt, who worked for the League of Nations. Mundt hired Arendt to work temporarily for the League's Labour Department in the bureau of international travel as a recording secretary. She was so good at her job that she was also hired by the Jewish Agency to record Yiddish speeches, but she did not want to remain in Geneva. Anders and Blumenfeld had gone to Paris, and after a few months she left to join them once she had arranged for her mother's safe return to Königsberg.

6

'We Refugees'

When Arendt arrived in Paris she knew little French and was without papers, which meant she could not rent an apartment or find employment easily. Like many refugees, Arendt and Anders moved from hotel to hotel. Their first address was 5e, 9 rue Toullier, Hôtel Soufflot. The first job she was able to secure was at the 'Agriculture et Artisanat' on the Champs-Elysées. The Artisanat was run by the French politician Justin Godart, the head of the France-Palestine Committee. They offered young Jewish refugees training in farming and craftwork to prepare them for life on the land. Arendt coordinated evening lectures on Jewish history, Hebrew and Zionism, in addition to organizing clothing, medication and documents for students to emigrate.

Arendt used her position at the Artisanat to hire fellow Jewish émigrés, including Chanan Klenbort, the Yiddish poet and writer, who would become a lifelong friend. Klenbort was not a Zionist, but he was a political activist, and Arendt paid him to give her Hebrew and Yiddish lessons. When he asked her why she wanted to learn Hebrew and Yiddish, she told him: 'I want to know my people.' It was important to Arendt to learn the languages of her people, because she 'wanted to do practical work. Only Jewish work.' In a letter written later to her second husband Heinrich Blücher, Arendt proudly boasted that she was the only German Jew at the World Zionist conference who knew Yiddish.[1]

The position also allowed Arendt to support Günther Anders while he worked on his novel *Die molussische Katakombe* (The Molussian

Catacombs), a satire about a fascist utopia, which Bertolt Brecht saved after it was confiscated and returned by the Gestapo. When the officials took it, they only looked at the cover, which depicted a map of a magical fascist island. Brecht gave the novel to Anne Mendelssohn, who wrapped it in cheesecloth and hung it in the attic with some smoked ham. Arendt carried the book disguised as bacon as she travelled from Berlin, to Prague, to Geneva and finally Paris.[2]

In exile Arendt became acquainted with the existentialist philosophers Jean-Paul Sartre, Simone de Beauvoir and Albert Camus, and spent many hours in a café on the street where she lived with Arnold Zweig and Bertolt Brecht. Anne Mendelssohn moved to Paris and married Eric Weil; Hans Jonas visited them and they spent time with Anders's distant cousin Walter Benjamin. Arendt and Anders had met Benjamin in Berlin, but did not get to know him, despite living a short distance apart. Benjamin had fled Berlin around 18 March 1933, and spent a couple of weeks in Paris before travelling to Ibiza for several months, then Nice, before returning to Paris in October 1933. When Arendt and Benjamin met in Paris, he was writing *A Berlin Chronicle* and *Berlin Childhood Circa 1900*. Unlike Arendt, Benjamin was familiar with Paris. He had lived there on and off for years and had thought of moving there permanently, despite Gershom Scholem's attempts to get him to relocate to Palestine.

Arendt's relationship with Benjamin had a lasting influence on her life and work. She attended his talk 'The Author as Producer' at the Institut pour l'Étude du Fascisme on 27 April 1934, which was written as a companion piece to his work on epic theatre, addressing the relationship between authorship and politics. Together, the refugees in exile formed a thriving intellectual community. Sartre, Georges Bataille, Raymond Aron, Maurice Merleau-Ponty, Alexandre Koyré, André Breton, Jacques Lacan, Arendt and Anders among others attended Alexandre Kojève's lectures on Hegel at the Ecole des Hautes Etudes.[3] Arendt was not impressed by Kojève's work on Hegel. She wrote to a friend, 'Kojève actually believes philosophy had come to an end with Hegel and acted on the belief. He never wrote a book, even the Hegel book was not actually written by him.' Arendt did not agree with Kojève's reading of Hegel, which was influenced by Heidegger, but she saw its importance in centring the master–slave dialectic as the core of Hegel's *The Phenomenology of Spirit* (1807), and taught Kojève's work when she gave seminars on Hegel later in life.

In November 1934 Arendt applied for help from the Academic Assistance Council, which was founded in May 1933 by William Beveridge to assist academics who were forced to flee Nazi Germany in finding teaching posts in Britain and other countries.

Arendt in a Paris café, 1930s.

Arendt in Paris, *c.* 1935.

On Arendt's paperwork she listed her research fields as: 'History of Christianity till Augustine, Social History of German literature from Lessing till 1848, History of Jewish Emancipation and History of Antisemitism.' She wrote that she was a Liberal Jew, who could read English fluently, but had no practice speaking, and ordered her countries of preference as: England, United States of America, Palestine. She included her curriculum vitae and the letters of recommendation Karl Jaspers, Martin Heidegger, Martin Dibelius and Arnold Zweig had written for her fellowship with the Notgemeinschaft der Deutschen Wissenschaft to fund her habilitation. It appears from the available records that they tried to place Arendt at the London School of Economics and Political

Sciences (LSE). Karl Mannheim wrote a letter to the LSE saying that he had known Arendt since she was a student of his in Heidelberg and Frankfurt. Mannheim's words echoed the other letters: 'Dr. Arendt is one of the most gifted persons among the younger generation.' He implored them to help her finish her work.

But the offer did not come, and Arendt remained in Paris. Later, in 1942, on her application to receive aid from the Emergency Committee in Aid of Displaced Foreign Scholars in America, she described her nearly eight years in Paris:

> Apart from practical social work, I succeeded to resume my scientific work and to finish a biography of Rahel Varnhagen as a case study of the problematic conditions of Jewish assimilation in Germany. I collected material for a history of anti-semitism and lectured on this topic in different French Clubs and Societies and at the 'Deutsche Hochschule' (for refugees) in Paris.[4]

After some time working for the Agriculture et Artisanat, Arendt was hired by the Baroness Germaine de Rothschild to oversee her contributions to Jewish charities, investigate possible recipient organizations, and make sure her money was being put to proper use. Arendt was liked by the Rothschilds, but she did not like them. She thought they were parvenus, the worst kind of Jews – social climbers without any real political consciousness. Rothschild's favourite charity was a children's home, and 'she liked to appear in jewels and silks of the Rothschild's red, with her limousine full of toys and candies', so that the children would feel like 'they had been singled out for a miracle'.[5] Arendt spoke disparagingly about the Baroness, who remained unaware of her disdain.

Arendt's distinction between pariah and parvenu emerged from her work on Rahel Varnhagen. In her 1943 essay 'We Refugees', written for the small Jewish journal *Menorah*, Arendt returns to this distinction, drawing a sharp line between pariahs and parvenus.

In 'We Refugees' Arendt describes a Mr Cohn to illustrate the parvenu's persona. Mr Cohn was based upon an experience she had in Paris during the war years. A man had founded an émigré society 'in which German Jews asserted to each other that they were already Frenchmen. In his first speech Mr Cohn said: "We have been good Germans in Germany and therefore we shall be good Frenchmen in France."'[6] Arendt was horrified by the audience's resounding applause.

For Arendt, an outsider must consciously embrace their pariah status and carry their otherness with them through the world. In her rejection of the parvenu's optimism to start over, she praises the pariah who remains conscious of their identity, regardless of where they find themselves. The pariah's refusal to forget is a way of acknowledging the losses they must bear: 'A man who wants to lose his self discovers, indeed, the possibilities of human existence, which are infinite, as infinite as is creation. But the recovering of a new personality is as difficult – and as hopeless – as a new creation of the world.'[7] In an attempt to cast off their past, parvenus try to forget who they are. But, for Arendt, such forgetting is not possible. They must carry their identity with them through the world, even if that means they are an outsider.

Arendt spent a few months with the Rothschilds before leaving to work as the General Secretary of Youth Aliyah in France in 1935. Similar to the Artisanat, Youth Aliyah was a Zionist organization that helped prepare and send Jewish youth to Palestine to live on *kibbutzim*, collective communities traditionally based on agriculture. The organization had been founded in Berlin in 1933 by Recha Freier as a response to the rise of the Third Reich. Arendt wrote a short essay, 'Some Young People Are Going Home', about her work for Youth Aliyah, where she reflected upon the ethical dimensions of Aliyah (Hebrew for 'migration to Israel'), and what it means to be at home in the world when one is rendered homeless:

Jews have been wandering around the world for two thousand years, taking in tow their belongings, their children, and their nostalgia for a homeland. They often lose their possessions in foreign countries. And what do they gain? The experience of sadness – the faculty of adapting and not letting themselves be annihilated. But children, not yet capable of fully understanding this destiny, lose everything: a stable household, a normal environment, their homeland, their friends, and their language. Not only are they uprooted, they are soon led astray.[8]

In 1935 Youth Aliyah sent Arendt to Palestine for three months with a group of trainees who were ready to emigrate. They took the train from the Gare de Lyon to Marseilles, and then boarded a ship to Haifa, stopping in Sicily and Greece on the way. Arendt took her group of students to the Sicilian city of Syracuse to see the historic ruins there, a site to which she returned several times throughout her life. She visited Ernst Fürst, her cousin from Königsberg, and his wife Käthe in Jerusalem, toured the city and travelled to Petra in the south, where she saw her first Roman temple.

Despite Arendt's Zionism during the war years, she was never interested in moving to Palestine or pursuing Zionism as a political doctrine. Arendt was a Zionist for political reasons. The Jewish people needed a homeland. She recalled her 1935 trip to Palestine in a letter later written to Mary McCarthy in 1967: 'I still remember my first reaction to the *kibbutzim* very well. I thought: a new aristocracy. I knew even then that one could not live there.'[9]

As Arendt became more involved with the Zionist movement, Anders tried to make a living as an independent writer. But by the mid-1930s their marriage had become more of a practical partnership. They lived together, shared meals together and met with friends when they weren't working, but at home they had romantically drifted apart. When Anders fled Berlin, their bond broke, but the reality was that it was never very strong to begin with. Those who knew them commented on how outmatched he was by her intellect and independence, but Anders had failed to notice the gap that grew between them. Arendt's friend Hans Jonas said, 'Hannah quickly became a well-respected figure among the Parisian émigrés . . . Günther stood along and began to play the role of the princely consort, which, as an ambitious and vain man, made him difficult to bear.'[10] Arendt confessed to friends that she had never really loved him, and only married him indifferently because she had no expectations for marriage.[11] Arendt had wanted to divorce Anders for some time, but was reluctant to leave him. 'My only option,' she wrote, 'was passive resistance, termination of all matrimonial duties.'[12]

When Stern left for America in June 1936, they decided to separate for good, filing divorce papers the same month:

The parties are separated since June, 1936: the last relations they had – Summer, 1933. The Plaintiff petitions for a divorce, as the Defendant has maintained illegal relations with another woman in New York. She has in her possession a letter of the Defendant of February 18, 1937. Among other things it says: 'It would be better if you did not make any use of the American visa and do not come, as we have agreed in New York. It would create an unbearable situation for you, as well as for me. You are right in your statement: I do not live alone. I have found a woman, with whom I am together. I wouldn't want to give her up.'[13]

Their divorce was finalized on 18 September 1937. It is not clear that Anders had actually taken up with another woman, but it is clear that he was never the great love of Arendt's life. And just as Arendt had been consciously aware of Heidegger's distance, Anders was aware of Arendt's. She did not hold any ill-feelings towards him, but he held on to a kind of bitterness about their marriage until the end of his life, which is apparent in the little book he wrote about their time together.

Arendt was not alone for long. She met Heinrich Friedrich Ernst Blücher in the early spring of 1936 at a public lecture, while she was still technically married to Anders. Blücher was a communist who had been involved in the Spartacist uprisings, and played a serious role in Berlin's left-wing Marxist movement. He had fled to Paris from Berlin by way of Prague in 1934, and like Anders was friends with Bertolt Brecht, Walter Benjamin and the left-wing intellectual circle in Paris. Unlike Anders, he was born into a poor, working-class family, had never received a formal education, and wasn't Jewish. He was auto-didactic, well read, charming and what one might call a *Lüftmensch* – there was a bit of airiness about him. On his German identity forms he listed *Drahtzieher* (stringpuller) as his profession. It was one of his code names in the Communist Party.[14]

Hannah Arendt's friends were much more favourable to Blücher than they had been to Anders. Hans Jonas reflected that 'theirs was a genuinely loving marriage'.[15] A friend of Arendt's, the writer Alfred Kazin, recalled that Blücher was a fantastic talker with a hypnotic style, although you were not always sure what he said. Hermann Broch remarked on his 'unstoppable flow of oratory brilliance', after recounting a lecture Blücher had given him until three in the morning, after Arendt had gone to bed. The American writer and philosopher Dwight Macdonald remembers him as 'a true, hopeless anarchist both in mind and in thought'.

Some time passed after their initial meeting before a supper was arranged by their mutual friend Chanan Klenbort at Hannah Arendt's apartment. When Blücher arrived in suit and hat, carrying a walking stick, Arendt playfully began calling him 'Monsieur'. Blücher pretended to be a bourgeois tourist during the day so that he would not appear to be a refugee in exile. Their supper, their

Heinrich Blücher in Paris, 1930s.

first official meeting, lasted until two in the morning. Each time Klenbort tried to leave he was persuaded to stay, until finally Arendt ended the evening and dismissed both men at the same time. After they were married, Arendt would often joke that their courtship had been one evening's duration. After a couple of weeks of seeing each other Blücher told her: 'You are in love with me and we will be married, but you don't know it yet.' By the end of the summer of 1936 Arendt and Blücher were living together on the rue de la Convention and had begun calling each other husband and wife.

Blücher was not a traditional academic and he did not fashion himself as an intellectual. He wasn't interested in publishing or writing even, so much as he was interested in ideas. He told Arendt that at his birth he had been blessed and cursed, by a good fairy who had given him a good brain, and by a bad fairy, who had given him writer's block. The son of a communist and laundress, Blücher had come to his political awakening on the streets of Berlin during the First World War. He was a self-made man with a voracious appetite for conversation and women. For the first two years of their relationship, while they were living together in Paris, Arendt did not know he was married. She found out about his wife, Natasha Jefroikyn, by accident while working for Youth Aliyah, when a man named Israel Jefroikyn came to work for the organization. One afternoon he was telling Arendt about his sister's wonderful husband when, to Arendt's surprise, she realized that he was talking about Heinrich Blücher. Blücher had married Jefroikyn in 1932, and they had lived together on and off until the autumn of 1935.[16] The discovery, though surprising, did not shake Arendt's relationship with Blücher: she had still been married when they met, and together they agreed to finalize their divorces.

Over time Arendt and Blücher came to know one another through conversation. With him she found a sense of place in the world. She called him her 'four walls' and 'portable home'. Theirs was 'an intellectual marriage of the passions'. Blücher once said,

'We each do our work, and then come together to discuss.' The erotic attraction between them was nourished by their intellectual connection. In an early love letter, Arendt writes:

> when I met you, suddenly I was no longer afraid – after that first fright, which was just a childish fright pretending to be grown up. It still seems incredible to me that I managed to get both things, the 'love of my life' and a oneness with myself. And yet, I only got the one thing when I got the other. But finally I also know what happiness is.[17]

When Arendt had travelled to Palestine a few years earlier, she had been struck by the durability of the Roman ruins, how they had remained amidst so much catastrophe. In her study of Roman politics she found the sacredness of foundation, and the courage of commitment, both of which were necessary for freedom in the world. In Heinrich Blücher she found another sense of durability that gave her the freedom to pursue her work.

In the spring of 1939 Arendt asked Chanan Klenbort's wife Lotte to go to Königsberg and help her mother move to Paris. It was not safe for Martha to be in Königsberg, and her marriage with Martin Beerwald had dissolved during the late 1930s. Martha filed her paperwork for emigration in April 1939 with the police and the financial authorities in Königsberg, and was granted a three-month visa to emigrate to France on condition that she surrender all items of value, except for a knife, fork, tablespoon, teaspoon, personal wristwatch and wedding rings. Martha left Königsberg on 24 April 1939 and arrived in France the next day.

7

Internment

On 1 September 1939 Nazi Germany invaded Poland. During the interwar period, France had adopted an open-door policy, welcoming Jewish immigrants mostly from eastern Europe. But by 1939 the French authorities had decided to impose strict limitations on immigration to deal with the rapid arrival of refugees fleeing Germany and the Spanish Civil War. They began building internment and detention camps for refugees, and decrees were issued to regulate the 'alien' population, prohibiting them from opening businesses, demanding the repatriation of unregistered Jews, and the expulsion of Jewish people without work permits. The influx of refugees had led to an increase in anti-Semitic sentiment among the French population.

France and England declared war against Germany on 3 September, and the same day placards were posted around Paris ordering German and Austrian male citizens to report to the Olympic stadium in the northwestern suburb of Colombes. Heinrich Blücher, Walter Benjamin, the playwright Hermann Kesten and the poet Hans Sahl, among others, reported for internment in the first round of mass detainments. For ten days they were fed cheap liver pâté on bread and slept on the ground of the open-air stadium, until they were divided into groups and sent to internment camps across France. Blücher and Benjamin were transported to Gare d'Austerlitz, then sent by train to Nevers, 240 kilometres (150 mi.) south of Paris. When they arrived they were forced to march for two hours to the abandoned Château de Vernuche.[1]

Blücher spent nearly two months in the camp with three hundred other prisoners. The abandoned château had been completely emptied out, and when they arrived it was dark and damp. After a couple of days they were given straw to sleep on. What information they received came through letters and loved ones, who were allowed to visit on Sundays at 12:00 p.m. for 30 minutes. Arendt baked cakes for Blücher and took him care packages.

Her letters to Blücher from this time did not survive the war, but 23 of Blücher's letters written in French remain, detailing his time in the camp. They mostly discuss his struggles with kidney stones and illness, which left him in bed for weeks at a time. He tries to reassure Arendt, telling her how nice the guards had been, and how the doctor was trying to heal him. He writes, 'My sweet, do your best. I will do my best, too. It is good to be able to think about you under stars.' He asked her for red wine, cigarettes and chocolate, the common currency of the camp. In one letter, Blücher sends Arendt a list:

I need:
1. My ski boots.
2. My winter jacket.
3. Trousers (Manchester velvet, beige or brown)
4. My winter socks.
5. 2 shirts.
6. A stainless steel kitchen knife (not a pointed one!).
7. Mess tin.
8. . . . to wash my head.
9. My small pipe (the one you gave me as a present.)
10. My tobacco pouch.

The horizon of the future was foreclosed in the camp. With little news from the outside, they were left with the toil of daily life inside. In Arendt's essay on Bertolt Brecht in *Men in Dark Times* (1968), she recounts a story about a poem of Brecht's that Walter Benjamin had brought back to Paris from Denmark:

> This poem had not yet been published when, at the beginning of the war, the French government decided to put its refugees from Germany in concentration camps, but in the spring of 1939, Walter Benjamin had brought it back to Paris from a visit to Brecht in Denmark, and speedily, like a rumor of good tidings, it traveled by word of mouth – a source of consolation and patience and endurance – where such wisdom was most needed.[2]

Arendt memorized the poem by heart, and Blücher took their copy with him and read it to the other detainees. The poem, 'Legend of the Origin of the Book Tao-te Ching during Lao-tse's Journey into Exile', is a reflection on dark times. In Arendt's essay on Brecht, written after the war, she notes how there was no attempt at playfulness in 'language or thought'. Instead, Brecht's poem was a form of lesson on 'nonviolence and wisdom'.[3]

With the help of friends, Blücher was released in the winter of 1940 with a letter from a doctor testifying to his chronic medical problems. Shortly after, he and Arendt decided to get married in a Parisian civil court on 16 January 1940, but the joy of their new marriage was cut short. Four months after their wedding, on 5 May 1940, an announcement was issued in the newspapers by the Governor General of Paris that all men between the ages of 17 and 55, and unmarried or childless married women who had come from Germany, the Saarland or Danzig, were to report for transport to internment camps.

Arendt and Blücher were sent to separate camps. The men were to report on 14 May at the Stadion Buffalo and the women on 15 May at the Vélodrome d'Hiver between 9 a.m. and 5 p.m. They were instructed to carry food sufficient for two days, their own eating utensils and sacks or suitcases weighing no more than 30 kilograms (90 lb). Arendt left her mother with Chanan Klenbort, and travelled to the rail station with her friend Franze Neumann and two other women. Many had arranged to travel together and had met up in Paris in small groups before taking the train to the stadium from Gare de Lyon. When the women arrived at the Vélodrome they were forced to line up for a medical screening to determine whether or not they were fit for labour. The streets surrounding the Vélodrome were packed with women standing in line, waiting to pass through the screening process. As they stood there, policemen walked up and down giving orders: 'It is forbidden to bring knives, scissors, or cigarettes with you.'[4]

Around five o'clock, it began to pour. Several thousand women stood in the rain, waiting to be inspected. The policemen, unsure of what to do, panicked and ran up and down the lines telling them to rush inside. The women were assigned places on the concrete benches and divided into groups of four to prevent mass protest. They ate dried, salted fish, slept on straw sleeping sacks, and were given tin cans to use as latrines. There were air raid sirens day and night with no shelter overhead. After about two weeks the women were loaded onto buses and taken to Gare d'Austerlitz. From there they were packed into train cars and transported to camps.[5]

Around 25 May the women arrived at Gurs. The camp was a large stretch of bare earth, partitioned into thirteen sections – *îlots* (islands) – which were enclosed with barbed wire, and ordered by letters of the alphabet. Three hundred wooden barracks were built in the camp to house 20,000 people. The barracks were about 30 metres (100 ft) long and 7 metres (22 ft) wide, with doors at either end. The ground was a swamp in the spring rain and the mud made it impossible to move about. The camp was supervised by non-Jewish female prisoners. Lisa Fittko, who offers the most detailed description of Gurs in her *Escape through the Pyrenees* (2000), describes them as sex workers. Others describe them as political refugees who were imprisoned as enemy aliens. The camp workers were appointed to oversee their fellow prisoners, and instructed the women in daily routines and tasks to keep them busy. The chores were meant to prevent despair. In *Vivre à Gurs* (Living in Gurs), Hanna Schramm describes how the women arriving 'looked like ghosts, confused and bewildered, in an unfamiliar world'.[6] Between the mud, pollution, lack of shelter and food, the conditions in Gurs were horrendous.

When Arendt arrived at Gurs there were 2,364 women and by 29 June that number had nearly doubled. They organized discussion groups and classes, from English lessons for those who hoped to receive American Emergency Visas, to lectures on philosophy. One survivor writes,

> The food was minimal, totally inadequate to say the least – ersatz coffee, slices of black bread . . . We can't remember receiving real solid food. We were given watery soup in which a few cabbage leaves floated. The lucky ones found a lump of potato or carrot in their ladle of soup . . . We were always hungry.[7]

At night the women who died from dysentery, and the women who were murdered by guards, were buried in the farthest rear corner of the camp.

After the French armistice with Germany in June 1940, Gurs fell under the authority of the Vichy regime. By October 1940 the German authorities had deported 7,500 Jewish people from southwestern Germany across the border into France, and interned them in Gurs. A total of 1,710 people were eventually released; 755 escaped; 1,940 were able to emigrate; and 2,820 men were conscripted into French labour battalions. By 1941, however, there were 15,000 people interned in Gurs. And in 1942 and 1943, under the direction of Adolf Eichmann, the remaining Jewish people were sent to Auschwitz via Drancy and murdered upon arrival. When the Vichy regime closed Gurs in November 1943, only 735 women, 250 men and 215 children remained.[8]

Hannah Arendt never discussed the details of her internment. There are only three instances in her work where she reflects upon this time. In 'We Refugees' (1947) she writes:

> At the camp of Gurs where I had the opportunity of spending some time, I heard only once about suicide, and that was the suggestion of a collective action, apparently a kind of protest in order to vex the French. When some of us suggested that we had been shipped there *pour crever* [to be done in] in any case, the general mood turned suddenly into a violent courage for life. The general opinion held that one had to be abnormally asocial and unconcerned about general events if one was still able to interpret the whole accident as personal and individual bad luck, and, accordingly, ended one's life personally and individually.[9]

In Arendt's preface to *The Origins of Totalitarianism* (1951) she echoes the same hesitation about reckless optimism and despair. For Arendt they are two sides of the same coin, turning people's gaze away from the present, towards the past and future. Arendt illustrates what she means in an essay titled 'The Destruction of Six Million', in which she looks to the Polish poet Tadeusz Borowski to express her political frustration with hope and despair. Born in 1922, Borowski was only a teenager when he was captured and sent to Auschwitz and then Dachau. He was liberated from Dachau on 1 May 1945 by u.s. troops: six years later he took his own life by putting his head in a gas oven. In his collection of short stories and poems, *This Way for the Gas, Ladies and Gentlemen*, Borowski captures what Arendt means by reckless despair and optimism:

> Never before in the history of mankind has hope
> been stronger than man, but never also has it done so

much harm as it has in this war, in this concentration
camp. We were never taught how to give up hope, and
this is why today we perish in gas chambers.[10]

For Borowski, giving up hope meant rejecting life for life's sake.
Hope was not hope for a better world, but for life itself. It was a
hope for a return to a world before concentration camps. It was
a hope that what they once had might be restored. From this
quotation, Arendt describes how 'hope' becomes a dangerous
barrier to life that breaks down the importance of social ties and
human relationships. When hope prevents action, and optimism
forces individuals to turn back upon themselves away from the
world, not only does the distinction between public and private life
collapse, but humanity is extinguished.

The second record of Arendt's internment comes from a letter
she wrote to her friend Kurt Blumenfeld in August 1952. Thinking
about despair, Arendt tells him: 'if only world history were not so
awful, it would be a joy to live. But, then, that is the case anyway.
At least, that was my opinion in Gurs where I posed the question
to myself in earnest and answered myself somewhat jokingly.'[11]
The question was suicide, but Arendt decided against it. For her,
personal responsibility outweighed collective experience. But it was
a serious question, and her response – 'jokingly' – was testament
to its gravity. Discussing Adolf Eichmann years later she said,
'Tragedy deals with the sufferings of mankind in a less serious way
than comedy.'

The final and most explicit account appears a decade later,
in a review of Bruno Bettelheim's essay 'Freedom from Ghetto
Thinking', written for the magazine *Midstream* in 1962:

I was 5 weeks in Gurs (not 2 days); we had been put there by
the regular French government during the last weeks of the
war as 'enemy aliens'. A few weeks after our arrival in the

camp – which was a regular concentration camp, originally
built for the soldiers of the Spanish Republican army – France
was defeated and all communications broke down. In the
resulting chaos, we succeeded in getting hold of liberation
papers with which we were able to leave the camp. There existed
no French underground at the time, of course (the French
resistance movement sprang up much later, namely when
the Germans decided to draft Frenchmen for forced labor in
Germany whereupon many young people went into hiding
and then formed the maquis). None of us could 'describe' what
lay in store for those who remained behind. All we could do
was to tell them what we expected would happen – the camp
would be handed over to the victorious Germans. (About
200 women of a total of 7,000 left.) This happened indeed,
but since the camp lay in what later became Vichy-France, it
happened years later than we expected. The delay did not help
the inmates. After a few days of chaos, everything became
very regular again and escape was almost impossible. We
rightly predicted this return to normalcy. It was a unique
chance, but it meant that one had to leave with nothing but a
toothbrush since there existed no means of transportation.[12]

The only first-hand account we have of Arendt's internment
comes from Lisa Fittko, who helped organize the mass escape.
In *Escape through the Pyrenees* Fittko describes how the women
managed to flee during a moment of chaos. News was prohibited
inside the camps, but occasionally a newspaper would be smuggled
in. On 14 June a paper appeared announcing: 'German Troops
March Through Paris.' Upon hearing the news, they began
planning their escape immediately:

> Camp discipline seemed to fall apart. The sentries, the
> officers, even the *commissaire spécial de police* – all of them

were confused and distraught. They had lost their orientation because there were no guidelines; order broke down, for there were no orders to follow. It was possible to slip out of your own *îlot*, a block with nearly a thousand human beings in it, and visit people in another *îlot*. Often the sentries weren't at their posts; they seemed scarcely to see any of us. We started to set up a news network, thin and fragile as it was. Only the *îlot des indésirables* was still under heavy guard.[13]

In the days leading up to the escape a woman in the camp was recruited to forge fake exit documents. She had specialized in forgery under Hitler, and was skilled enough to replicate the commander's signature. For the next few days she made certificates from morning to night, often with the other women hovering over her.

They did not know what was going to happen, but they knew that with the German advance they would be sent elsewhere. Assuming there would be a transition period between the German occupation and retreat of the French guards, they made a plan to escape using the forged papers. As confusion in the camp increased from hour to hour, they were able to move freely between the once heavily guarded islands and begin distributing the certificates. They gave one to Hannah Arendt, who was part of the underground news network set up inside the camp. They met at 8:00 a.m. on the left side of the gate and agreed to pass through singly or in twos. They showed the guard the forged certificates only if asked, and walked out of the camp gate. They left the unused certificates behind for those who decided to try and leave. Arendt insisted on walking out alone.

8

State of Emergency

When Arendt escaped the Gurs internment camp in the middle of June 1940 she went to Lourdes to find Walter Benjamin. Lourdes is about 70 kilometres (43 mi.) southeast of Gurs. Most of the women were travelling in groups, walking and hitchhiking, but Arendt insisted on making the journey alone; she thought it was safer than travelling in a group.[1]

In a letter written to Gershom Scholem on 17 October 1941, Arendt recounts her time with Benjamin:

> As soon as I got out of Gurs in the middle of June, by chance I, too, headed to Lourdes, where I stayed for a few weeks at his instigation. This was the time of defeat, and after a few days the trains stopped running. No one knew what had happened to families, husbands, children, and friends. Benji and I played chess from morning to evening, and between games we read newspapers, to the extent that we could get our hands on them.[2]

When Benjamin was released from the Clos St Joseph camp in Nevers in the spring of 1940, he returned to Paris for a brief period before fleeing to Lourdes around 14 June while he waited for his visa papers to the United States to arrive in Marseilles. Benjamin had been spared a second internment in the spring of 1940 by intervention of the French poet and diplomat St John Perse, because of his poor health.

At the beginning of July Arendt hesitantly left Benjamin to look for her husband, Heinrich Blücher. She considered taking Benjamin with her, but decided it would have been impossible.[3] He remained in Lourdes, waiting for word from Max Horkheimer and Theodor Adorno at the Institute for Social Research, which was operating in exile in New York, about his exit papers. Arendt walked and hitchhiked to Montauban, where Lotte Klenbort, the wife of her good friend Chanan Klenbort, had rented a house. Montauban was a meeting point for refugees, and Arendt arrived not knowing where Blücher was, but hopeful that she would receive word of his whereabouts. No messages, however, arrived. Until, one day, fate intervened. Walking down the main thoroughfare, where people went to look for food, cigarettes and newspapers, they ran into each other. The Nevers internment camp where Blücher had been held was evacuated when Paris fell to the Germans. The French guards had started to move the detainees south, but when the Germans appeared they released the men and fled. Blücher had hitchhiked his way from Nevers to Montauban to be treated for an inner-ear infection.[4]

When they reunited, Arendt and Blücher rented a small apartment above a photographer's studio in town and began looking for exit papers. While they waited, Arendt read Proust's *Remembrance of Things Past* (1913), Carl von Clausewitz's *On War* (1832) and the detective stories of Georges Simenon. Blücher read Immanuel Kant.[5] In October, with the tightening of the Vichy regime, all Jewish people were required to register with the local prefects. Arendt's mother, Martha, travelled to Montauban from Paris and together they took several trips to Marseilles in search of papers. Arendt refused to register with the prefects' office to comply with the police orders, knowing that the lists were being used to arrest refugees. When word came that they would be able to secure papers, they left Montauban and made their way to Marseilles by bicycle.

Hannah Arendt, her mother and Heinrich Blücher were able to secure their visas with the help of Varian Fry, who was the head of the Emergency Rescue Committee. Fry, a writer and journalist from New York, had travelled to Marseilles two months after the fall of France as a founder of the Committee to try to save as many Jewish artists, writers and thinkers as he could. As a reporter on foreign affairs, he had no legal experience, but learned how to obtain false passports and visas, and forged the paperwork necessary for organizing emigration. Before he was caught and expelled, Fry spent thirteen months in Marseilles and saved more than 2,000 people, including Jean Arp, Marc Chagall, Max Ernst, André Breton, Max Ophuls and Marcel Duchamp, among many others. [6]

But Arendt's dear friend Walter Benjamin did not make it. In August 1940 the Institute for Social Research was able to secure an American Emergency Visa for Benjamin. Upon receiving word, he travelled to Marseilles to wait for his visa to arrive at the American consulate. There he was reunited with Hannah Arendt and Heinrich Blücher. The last time Arendt saw Benjamin was in Marseilles on 19 September 1940. Benjamin took his own life six days later in Portbou, trying to cross the border into Spain. The report of his death took almost four weeks to reach her. What information exists about his final days comes from Lisa Fittko and Henny Gurland (the wife of psychologist and philosopher Erich Fromm), who led a small group of refugees through the Pyrenees to Portbou, a common path known as the Smuggler's Route. Fittko describes how Benjamin had to walk for ten minutes, then rest for ten minutes, given his poor health. He carried only a leather attaché case containing his most valuable papers. Upon arriving in Portbou on the night of 26 September they were told at the police station that the Spanish government had cancelled all transit visas, and that without French exit papers they would be returned and sent to camps. That night Benjamin took a lethal dose of morphine.

Walter Benjamin, 1934, photographed by Gisèle Freund.

Arendt and Blücher rented a hotel room in Marseilles and waited for a message to arrive telling them that they could go to the American consulate. Then one day a message was sent up to their room requesting Heinrich Blücher report to the front desk. Arendt and Blücher knew the call was a trick, and that the police could not be far behind. Playing innocent, Blücher went downstairs, left his key and walked out the front door before anyone could stop him. Arendt followed a bit after and they made their way to a café where Blücher could safely hide. Arendt went back to the hotel, paid the bill and ate breakfast. When the hotel clerk came over and asked her where her husband was, she staged a loud scene, shouting that he was already at the prefecture's office, telling the clerk he was responsible for whatever happened to her husband. She left the hotel, picked up Blücher from the café and together they left Marseilles.[7]

In January 1941 the Vichy government briefly relaxed its exit permit policy. Arendt and Blücher immediately travelled by train to Lisbon, stopping in Portbou on the way to look for Benjamin's grave. Arendt writes to Gershom Scholem:

> Months later, when we arrived at Portbou, we searched in vain for his grave. It was nowhere to be found. His name was nowhere. The cemetery faces a small bay, directly looking over the Mediterranean. It is carved in stone terraces; the coffins are also pushed into such stone walls. It is by far one of the most fantastically beautiful places I've ever seen.

In June 1941 the U.S. Department of State tightened its entry policy and of the 1,137 names submitted, only 238 received emergency visas to the United States between August and December 1941. Arendt and Blücher received two of them. After three months in Lisbon, they were free to leave for New York with the hope that Martha would follow close behind. In Arendt's absence, Nina Gourfinkel, a Russian Jewish writer who helped to provide housing for Jews and other displaced people, looked after Martha in Marseilles until her visa arrived and she too could leave for America.

As Arendt and Blücher sailed to New York they took what they had, including a suitcase of Walter Benjamin's last writings, which contained his *Theses on the Philosophy of History*. As they crossed the Atlantic, they read the *Theses* aloud to their fellow émigrés:

> The tradition of the oppressed teaches us that the 'state of emergency' in which we live is not the exception but the rule. We must attain to a conception of history that is in keeping with this insight. Then we shall clearly realize that it is our task to bring about a real state of emergency, and this will improve our position in the struggle against Fascism.[8]

Hannah Arendt was 35 years old when she boarded the ss *Guiné* for New York City. She had fled two world wars, been arrested by the Gestapo and escaped an internment camp. In her introduction to Benjamin's *Illuminations* she talks about misfortune: 'There is, however, another less objective element than the mere fact of being unclassifiable which is involved in the life of those who "have won victory in death". It is the element of bad luck.'[9] But Hannah Arendt was not subject to this element of bad luck. Fortune, that mysterious goddess, long considered by philosophers to be cruel in unpredictable ways, seemed to come to Arendt's aid when the chips were down.

9

Transition

Hannah Arendt and Heinrich Blücher arrived at Ellis Island in New York on 22 May 1941 with 25 dollars and very little English. They rented two furnished rooms at 317 West 95th Street with a stipend from the Zionist Organization of America. The 'List or Manifest of Alien Passengers for the United States' registers Heinrich Blücher as a 42-year-old, stateless, German writer, and Johanna Arendt as a 35-year-old, stateless, Hebrew wife.

The morning after their arrival, Arendt sent a telegram to her first husband, Günther Anders, letting him know they had made it:

1941 May 23 am 11 20: 'We're Saved. We are here
and living at 317 West 95th Street= HANNAH.'[1]

Martha arrived a few weeks later on 21 June on the ss *Mouzinho* and moved into the second room Arendt and Blücher had rented. Martha's friend Julie Braun-Vogelstein sent them packages of food and clothing from Königsberg.[2] Arendt's friend Paul Tillich, who had relocated to New York in 1933, put Arendt in touch with an organization called Self-Help for Refugees, an agency of the United Jewish Appeal-Federation of Jewish Philanthropies in New York. Through them, Arendt applied to be placed as a housekeeper with an American family for the summer to learn English. From 18 July to 15 August 1941 she worked in the Giduz home at 92 Arlington Street in Winchester, a few miles north of Boston. In her first letter to Blücher from Massachusetts, Arendt described her new living conditions:

> The little house my family lives in is really pretty, a kind of 'dwelling machine' with books. Winchester is an endlessly stretched out garden town consisting exclusively of one-family houses. Everyone who can in any way afford to (and even the simplest middle-class families, like mine, can) lives outside the working district. We live right at the edge of the woods. It's delightfully calm and quiet here. With the garden and everything else, there's so much work that (at least for the husband) the advantages of living in a 'dwelling machine' are canceled out.[3]

Despite the premise of Arendt's appointment, Mrs Giduz did not let her do much housekeeping. Arendt spent her days reading, studying and going for walks. The Giduzes bought her an English-German dictionary, and selected some books for her bedroom. She visited the Museum of Fine Arts and was impressed by the 'mass of beautiful things . . . particularly the Greek sculpture and marvelous vases'. She took in the Rembrandts and Manets, and attended the open-air concerts of the Boston Symphony. On the weekends they took her for long drives to explore the surrounding towns, and at night they stayed up talking about politics. At first Arendt had been slightly worried that they were pro-German, but she quickly realized they were pacifists, and Mr Giduz was a Polish Jew who had hidden his identity after his family emigrated to America.

Arendt took more quickly to Mr Giduz than Mrs Giduz, who was an avid vegetarian with an ascetic personality. 'She is ready to fight to the death for healthy nutrition. Healthy nutrition is: 1. No meat. 2. No fried fat (gallbladder diet). 3. Lots of vegetables, preferably raw. 4. No white bread.'[4] But Arendt and Mr Giduz found a way around Mrs Giduz's health regulations. When she left the home in the morning, they would start their day with bacon and eggs, and Arendt cooked them whole chickens for lunch. She wrote to Blücher, 'It was quite an achievement.' Her only lament was that she could not convince Mr Giduz into eating French fries with her.[5] Arendt found Mr Giduz more 'clever' and 'sensible' than his wife, though she was impressed with Mrs Giduz's sense of civic duty. One evening she watched her write angry letters to her Congressmen protesting the internment of Japanese Americans.

Arendt's early experiences in the Giduzes' home left a lasting impression on her sense of American politics. Arendt was interested in the myth of the American 'melting pot', and how Americans 'felt responsible for public life'. Hans Jonas writes,

> It was the experience of the Republic here which
> decisively shaped her political thinking . . . America
> taught her a way beyond the hardened alternatives of
> left and right from which she had escaped; and the idea
> of the Republic, as the realistic chance for freedom,
> remained dear to her even in its darkening days.[6]

What made the United States unique in Arendt's view was the fact that America had never been a nation-state, and so it was not 'affected by the vices of nationalism and chauvinism'. In America, she came to understand, citizenship was founded upon adherence to the constitution, not ethnicity or race.[7] She praised American federalism, the separation of powers and the lack of a centralized government.

Arendt had considered studying to become a social worker while she was in Massachusetts, but she decided against the idea. She wanted to return to her work, to Jewish politics and writing. She was happy about her time in Massachusetts and newfound education in American politics, but she did not forget what was happening in Europe, as she told Blücher: 'Newspapers and radio speeches here are giving a totally false picture, particularly when it comes to opinions on the war.'[8]

Heinrich Blücher had a more difficult time acclimatizing to life in America. He resisted learning English and only did so unhappily at the urging of Arendt. He spent his first year in the United States compiling a book of English idioms and working at a factory in New Jersey. He hated his job and left after a short time, when he was hired as a research assistant by the Committee for National Morale, which was an organization dedicated to urging America to enter the war. Arendt wrote to her friends Lotte and Chanan Klenbort, complaining that '*Monsieur* seldom got home before ten-o'clock at night'. Eventually Blücher found two teaching positions through his contacts at the Committee. As a civilian consultant for the u.s. Army Training Program at Camp Ritchie, Maryland, he conducted seminars on German history for German prisoners of war, and he was invited to lecture in the army program at Princeton University under the supervision of the Dean, Christian Gauss. The following year he was hired as a German-language news broadcaster for NBC radio.

After the summer Arendt went to Columbia University to visit the Jewish historian Salo Baron, whom she had met years earlier in Germany. During her meeting with Baron they talked about the history of anti-Semitism in France, and Baron suggested that she develop her argument into an article and send it to Theodor Herzl Gaster, who was the executive secretary for the Institute for Jewish Affairs. With his help, she published her first essay in English translation, 'From the Dreyfus Affair to France Today', in *Jewish Social Studies* in 1942.

Salo Baron and his wife Jeanette became close friends with Arendt and Blücher. In the reminiscences that Baron wrote for *Jewish Social Studies* shortly after her death, he recalls their first meeting:

I still vividly remember her first visit to my office at Columbia University soon after her arrival in this country. In discussing the Jewish situation in Vichy France, she evinced deep concern about the continuity of French antisemitism from Dreyfus to Petain . . . At the same time she was greatly intrigued by the fate of distinguished assimilated Jews who found themselves uprooted from their Jewish environment and yet did not become completely integrated into the national majorities of their respective countries.[9]

Arendt's second essay in *Jewish Social Studies* was published two years later. 'The Jew as Pariah: A Hidden Tradition' discussed the German poet Heinrich Heine, literary critic Bernard Lazare, Charlie Chaplin and Franz Kafka. She continued to write for *Jewish Social Studies*, but with Baron's help she also resumed her work in the Jewish community. Baron hired her as the Research Director at the Commission for Jewish Cultural Reconstruction, which he oversaw.

That autumn Arendt went to hear Kurt Blumenfeld give a lecture sponsored by *Aufbau* on the question: 'Should the Jews have an army?' *Aufbau* was the news bulletin for the German Club, a New York organization founded in 1924 to provide new emigrants with a meeting place. The paper sponsored discussions and lectures on current events, and over time it was transformed into a weekly paper that provided German Jewish émigrés with a forum for their political views. After Blumenfeld's lecture Arendt sent a letter to its editor, Manfred George, who invited her to submit an expanded version for publication. George was so impressed by her article he invited her to write a weekly column: 'This Means You'. Arendt used her column to call for the formation of a Jewish army to defend the Jewish people.

As Arendt began her new life in America, the war was growing more dire. On 7 December 1941 the Japanese bombed Pearl Harbor and the Imperial Japanese Navy assaulted the u.s. Pacific fleet, destroying eight battleships and killing 2,400 Americans. The next day the United States declared war on Japan, and three days later, on 11 December, Germany declared war on America. The United States was forced to enter the war in Europe, and that December news of the 'Final Solution' reached New York. The issue of *Aufbau* published on 18 December contained a list of names of those who had been deported from the Gurs internment camp to Auschwitz by Adolf Eichmann. In the National Socialist weekly *Das Reich*, Joseph Goebbels outlined the final solution outside of Germany and 'perhaps outside of Europe'. Arendt implored that immediate action must be taken:

> We who are alive have to learn that you can't live on your knees, that you don't become immortal by chasing after life, and that if you are no longer willing to die for anything, you will die for having done nothing. 'Not one mass will now be sung, not one Kaddish will be said.'[10]

Arendt continued writing for *Aufbau* and the following spring began organizing the Young Jewish Group with Joseph Maier and Kurt Blumenfeld. Their first meeting was held at the New World Club's 44th Street headquarters on 11 March 1942. Arendt announced the meeting in *Aufbau*:

> To those individuals who are convinced of the bankruptcy of past ideologies and ready to tear out their hair in order to develop a new theoretical basis for Jewish politics; to those who know that the struggle for freedom will be led neither by 'notables' nor by world-revolutionaries, but only by those who want to realize it for their own people; and to those who are truly prepared to answer for what they consider to be just.[11]

Arendt prepared a paper for the first meeting titled 'Basic Theoretical Questions of Politics'. Many of the ideas in this first paper, which called for a 'new theoretical basis for Jewish politics', appear in *The Origins of Totalitarianism, Between Past and Future* and *The Human Condition*. Arendt thought about the Jewish Question as a political question within the context of politics in general. For her, freedom was the primary principle of politics, and in order to protect spaces of freedom one must turn away from idealized notions of past and future. This turning away from past and future, towards the present, pushed against the Zionist line that was rooted in tradition. Arendt was a Zionist who was critical of Zionism. She regarded 'isms' as red flags for ideological thinking that attempted to move past the nuances of lived experience.

Arendt's relationship to Zionism changed after she emigrated to America. In Germany and Paris she had been an active Zionist, lecturing before Jewish audiences, sponsored by the organization B'nai B'rith, she arranged Hebrew courses, and travelled to Palestine. After she arrived in New York, she worked with Judah Magnes, who founded the Ikhud (Unity) party in Palestine, prepared a summary of the history of the Ikhud to present to the United Nations, and met with the UN Secretariat's appointee for political affairs. It was even suggested she serve on the committee representing the Ikhud, but she did not want to get involved in that kind of politics. In the United States Arendt was thrown into the crosshairs of competing Zionisms, which were structurally different from those she had known. In 1942 Arendt attended the Biltmore Conference with Joseph Maier, which irreversibly changed her relationship to Zionism. She was shocked by the atmosphere and the way she was treated because she refused to accept Prime Minister David Ben-Gurion's call for a Jewish state in Palestine.

Arendt's final essay for *Aufbau* was published on 20 November 1942. It was the last instalment of a three-part series on 'The Crisis of Zionism', which called upon dissident Zionists to accept the

Hannah Arendt at the Judah L. Magnes Foundation, New York, 18 December 1948.

idea that Palestine should not be a British colony, part of a colonial empire, in the manner outlined in the 1917 Balfour Declaration. Arendt supported the establishment of Palestine as part of a postwar British Commonwealth, rather than as an autonomous state. She thought that Gandhi's work in India could provide an example for a way forward. She also continued to advocate for a postwar European federation, because she thought that was the only way Palestine could be completely guaranteed as a *jüdisches Siedlungsgebiet* (area for Jewish settlements). She also made a plea for legislation that would classify anti-Semitism as a punishable crime against society within such a federation.[12] But in an atmosphere of growing enthusiasm for Ben-Gurion's Zionism, her suggestions were without effect, and her column was replaced in the next issue of *Aufbau* by one titled 'Zionistische Tribune'.

As Arendt told Günter Gaus in 1964, she was a Zionist from 1933 to 1943 because of the Jewish Question. But Arendt was never a nationalist, and she understood the nation to be a separate political entity from the state. She was attuned to the political dangers of anti-Semitism, but rejected the idea of 'eternal anti-Semitism', which is how Theodor Herzl spoke about Hitlerism. Arendt's early rejection of Nation-State Zionism resisted the idea that the Jewish people are a people united by a common enemy.

Arendt refused the ideological demands of Zionism. Her experiences as a Jewish person in the twentieth century were decisive for her turning to political thought from philosophy, in part because she saw the ways in which philosophy could circumscribe one's world-view. The Jewish Question for Arendt was always a political question. She writes at the beginning of *Origins*, 'It has been one of the unfortunate facts in the history of the Jewish people that only its enemies, and almost never its friends, have understood that the Jewish Question is a political one.'[13] Arendt thought that the Jewish people needed a homeland, but she was against founding a Jewish nation-state. In *Aufbau* she advocated for a European federation to guarantee a homeland for all Jewish peoples, so that they would have security when the nation-state system failed, as it had done so spectacularly in Europe. If the nation-state couldn't provide basic rights for all human beings, then for Arendt, it was our political obligation to fight for a political body that could. In *The Origins of Totalitarianism*, she formulated this principle as 'the right to have rights'. She wanted a Jewish front, and solidarity amidst Jewish peoples in different countries.[14]

10

Friendship

On 7 May 1945 the German armed forces surrendered in the West unconditionally. Hannah Arendt and Heinrich Blücher were at Salo Baron's country house in Connecticut on 8 May when victory in Europe was declared.

Arendt would spend the summer of 1945 in Hanover, New Hampshire, with her friend Julie Braun Vogelstein, working on *The Origins of Totalitarianism*, while following the news about what was happening in Europe. The end of the war meant that Arendt was able to reunite with friends. Hans Jonas had emigrated from Heidelberg to England in 1933, and then gone to Palestine in 1935. At the end of the war in 1945 he returned to Heidelberg briefly before deploying to Palestine as a soldier in the British Army's Jewish brigade. Anne Mendelssohn, who had married Eric Weil, a French-German philosopher, was in Paris working on the Marshall Plan at the French Ministry of Economic Affairs. Chanan and Lotte Klenbort had found refuge in Uruguay and were waiting to emigrate to the United States. Karl and Gertrud Jaspers had waited out the war in Heidelberg, which was occupied by the Americans on 1 April 1945.

Karl Jaspers wrote to Arendt that October after receiving a stack of her essays from Melvin Lasky, a leftist American journalist writing about military history in France and Germany who was visiting Heidelberg. Jaspers had been worried about Arendt, not knowing where she was, or if she had survived, and Arendt had been worried about Jaspers, too. Jasper's letter arrived like 'an outstretched hand', Arendt tells him: 'Ever since I've known that you both came through the whole hellish mess unharmed, I have felt somewhat more at home in this world again.'[1] She sent Jaspers and Gertrud letters and care packages of medicine, food, coffee, clothing, kosher sausage and American bacon with cooking instructions: 'Put the slices in a moderately hot pan and fry them over a low flame. Keep pouring the fat off until the slices are crisp. Then nothing can go wrong with either the fat or the bacon.'[2]

Friendship was an oasis for Arendt, and in dark times it offered a refuge. She said, in being with others, 'one heart reaches out directly to the other'. It is a meeting ground of equals, where one is free to go without a mask, without the pressures of performance and appearance. It is the intimacy of close relationships with others that teaches us how to breathe, to co-exist. Arendt scholar Kathleen B. Jones writes,

> For Arendt, friendship thrived on equality, but only in the sense of a shared commitment to independent thinking and a willingness to take risks. And despite her comparatively meager education, Fränkel possessed these qualities to an extraordinary degree. Her perceptive intelligence and her ability to talk frankly, though privately, about even her sexual life and erotic encounters endeared her to Arendt.[3]

Arendt's intimate circle, which she called her 'tribe', gave her a sense of home, and Arendt was discerning when it came to who she admitted to her tribe. Among those she let in were Hilde Fränkel, Paul Tillich's mistress. Tillich had introduced Arendt to Fränkel in Frankfurt during the 1930s when she was there with Anders. When the war began Fränkel had fled to Argentina with her family, but decided to emigrate to America in the 1940s. When Arendt reunited with Fränkel in New York, she was working as Tillich's secretary at Union Theological Seminary.

Arendt and Fränkel shared a deep intimacy and trusted one another. Before Fränkel died from cancer in 1950, Arendt wrote her long letters expressing her affection:

> I can hardly tell you how much I owe you, not only for the loosening up which comes from intimacy which comes from a woman like I have never have known before, but for the happiness of closeness, a happiness never to be lost, and all the greater since you aren't an 'intellectual' (what a hateful word), and therefore are a confirmation of myself and my true belief. I so long to talk with you and cannot imagine how I should live without you, incredibly impoverished, as if suddenly condemned to silence about the most important things when I have just learned to speak.[4]

Gertrude and Karl Jaspers in Basel, Switzerland, mid-1960s.

Mary McCarthy in Greece.

Before her passing, Fränkel entrusted Arendt with her will, to make
sure Tillich received a regular, small sum of money she wanted to
leave to him without his wife finding out. Frankel saw Arendt as a
kindred soul. With her she was able to speak fully and completely.
Frankel was not a writer, or even an intellectual, but she was
worldly, wise and 'gifted with erotic genius'. There was a sense of
womanly recognition between them that nourished and sustained
their friendship, allowing each a radical openness.

Arendt's circle of friends blossomed in New York as she began
to work in publishing. She spent time with Irving Howe, Nathan

Glazer, Dwight Macdonald, Hermann Broch, Hans Morgenthau, Helen and Kurt Wolff, W. H. Auden, Lionel and Diana Trilling, Robert Lowell, Elizabeth Hardwick, Lotte Kohler and Mary McCarthy.

Hannah Arendt first met McCarthy at the Murray Hill Bar in Manhattan in 1944. Arendt was being introduced to the critic Clement Greenberg by a co-worker from Schocken Books. 'McCarthy was struck by Arendt's skeptical wit' and 'electric vitality', and Arendt was 'filled with delight and wonder' at meeting Mary. At the time McCarthy was reviewing plays for *Partisan Review* and had published a collection of autobiographical fiction, *The Company She Keeps*. She was also at work translating Simone Weil's essay 'The Iliad or the Poem of Force' for Dwight Macdonald's journal *politics* and teaching Russian literature at Bard College in upstate New York.

They ran into each other again that spring at a party thrown by *Partisan Review* co-founder Philip Rahv. The second meeting, however, did not go as well as the first. In the middle of a conversation about the hostility of French citizens towards the Germans occupying Paris, McCarthy quipped, 'I feel sorry for Hitler.' According to McCarthy's account, Arendt exploded: 'How can you say such a thing to me, a victim of Hitler, a person who has been in a concentration camp!' And Arendt complained to Rahv: 'How can you have this kind of conversation in your home, you, a Jew?'

After that night Arendt and McCarthy did not talk for three years, until they were invited to meet with Macdonald to discuss *politics*.[5] They ran into one another on the subway platform after the meeting and Arendt said, 'We two think so much alike.' McCarthy apologized for her comment about Hitler, and Arendt told her she had never been in a concentration camp.

In the summer of 1945 Hannah Arendt received her first teaching position in the Graduate Division of Brooklyn College, lecturing on Modern European History, and a book contract for *The Origins of Totalitarianism*. She was working on articles, essays and book reviews for the *Partisan Review, Commentary, Menorah Journal* and the *Jewish Frontier*, many of which featured in *Origins*.

When Arendt first began writing in English she was attentive to the translation choices. During a panel interview from 1972, Arendt recounts one of her first experiences with an American editor at the *Partisan Review* who had 'Englished' an essay she wrote on Kafka:

> And when I came to talk to them about the Englishing I read the article and there of all things the word 'progress' appeared. I said: 'What do you mean by this, I never used that word,' and so on. And then one of the editors went to the other in another room, and left me there, and I overheard him say, in a tone of despair, 'She doesn't even believe in progress.'[6]

Arendt had an ear for language, she was attentive to valences and tones, the ways in which words worked together. When asked what remained after the war, she told Günter Gaus, 'the language remains', meaning the language of her mother tongue. More specifically, Arendt meant the language of German poetry that she carried around in her *hinterkopf* (the back of her mind). And when Arendt began to write in English she was influenced by American poets such as Randall Jarrell, to whom she would grow close.

Arendt and Jarrell met in 1945 after he arrived in New York to edit *The Nation*'s book review. As she recounts it,

> What brought us together was 'business' – I had been very impressed by some of his war poems and asked him to translate some German poems for the publishing house, and he edited (translated into English, I should say) some book reviews of mine for *The Nation*. Thus, like people in business, we made it a habit of lunching together, and these lunches, I suspect but do not remember, were paid for in turn by our employers; for this was still the time when we were all poor. The first

book he gave to me was *Losses*, and he inscribed it 'To Hannah (Arendt) from her translator Randall (Jarrell)', reminding me jokingly of his first name which I was slow to use, but not, as he suspected, because of any European aversion to first names; to my un-English ear Randall sounded not a bit more intimate than Jarrell, in fact, the two sounded very much alike.[7]

Their friendship was forged through poetry. Jarrell introduced Arendt to the work of English-language poets such as Emily Dickinson, Wordsworth, T. S. Eliot and W. B. Yeats, and Arendt helped Jarrell with his translations of German poems by Goethe, Rilke, Heine and Hölderlin. Through a shared love of language Jarrell helped Arendt craft her English writing style:

He read English poetry to me for hours, old and new, only rarely his own, which, however, for a time, he used to mail as soon as the poems came out of the typewriter. He opened up for me a whole new world of sound and meter, and he taught me the specific gravity of English words, whose relative weight, as in all languages, is ultimately determined by poetic usage and standards. Whatever I know of English poetry, and perhaps of the genius of the language, I owe to him.[8]

Arendt's fondness for Jarrell is documented in her essay on him in *Men in Dark Times*. She describes him in almost mystical terms as creating an atmosphere of magic, which commanded attention. With him she felt like she had been 'intoxicated with agreement against a world of enemies'.[9] While Jarrell was at *The Nation*, Arendt wrote five short pieces for the journal in 1946, including a review of Hermann Broch's *The Death of Virgil*, which Karl Jaspers had sent her from Heidelberg.

From 1946 to 1948 Arendt worked as an editor for Schocken Books, which Salman Schocken had founded in Berlin in 1931 and re-established in New York in 1945. Arendt liked the editorial work, but she had reservations about Schocken. In her letters with Jaspers, she called him the 'Jewish Bismarck'. Schocken had an imperious personality and, though he had consulted Arendt on a number of projects before hiring her, he refused to take on many of the authors she brought to him, including Walter Benjamin and Randall Jarrell. In one anecdote, Arendt recounted a meeting with T. S. Eliot, where Schocken treated him like a 'travelling salesman'. After speaking with him briefly, he stood up and abruptly left the room announcing that he would 'think it over'. Arendt sat in the corner of his office in silent horror, watching the scene unfold. When Schocken left, Eliot stood up, turned to Arendt and said, 'Well, now you and I can have a nice chat.'[10]

Among the works Arendt recommended Schocken take on was Bernard Lazare's *Job's Dungheap,* which was published in 1948, and Gershom Scholem's *Major Trends in Jewish Mysticism* (1941), which Arendt helped edit for American publication. Arendt also helped Schocken prepare the German edition of *Franz Kafka's Diaries* (1948–9), which Max Brod had edited for publication. Her job was to hand-check Brod's 'sloppy' work against Kafka's original papers. While Arendt was working on Kafka's diaries, she published an essay on his work in the *Partisan Review.*[11] Two versions of this essay were published in German, one a translation made for the Heidelberg journal *Die Wandlung,* and the other in her *Sechs Essays,* published in Heidelberg in 1948.[12]

Shortly before Arendt went to work for Schocken she was introduced to the Austrian modernist poet and writer Hermann Broch. Their initial meeting was arranged by Broch's second wife, Anne-Marie Meier-Gräfe. Arendt was immediately taken with Broch. With his sharp features and boyish smile, Broch, like Arendt's husband Blücher, was a bit of a Lothario. When he attempted to seduce Arendt, she implored him, 'Hermann, let me be the exception.' Arendt's refusal did not impede their friendship.

Hermann Broch, 1935.

In Arendt's review of *The Death of Virgil* (1945), she discusses Broch's temporal schema as the 'no longer and not yet'. Arendt thought that Broch's *Virgil* bridged the gap between Proust and Kafka. She wrote that the character of Virgil tried to span the abyss of empty space between the 'no longer' being of the world that had disappeared, and the 'not yet' of the world to come. The abyss, as Arendt saw it, which opened in 1914 with the beginning of the First World War, had not closed. Instead, it had only grown 'deeper and more frightful' until the death factories finally severed the thread.[13] This idea in Broch's reading of Virgil, together with Arendt's reading of Proust and Kafka, informed her conception of 'The Gap Space' in her work *Between Past and Future* (1954).

But Arendt's friendship with Broch was cut short by his unexpected death in the spring of 1951 from a heart attack. Arendt wrote to Alred Kazin:

> Broch's death was a sudden and deep shock – He belonged even more to my world than I had realized while he was still alive. I last saw him two days before his death – in my office where he used to come and fetch me for a cup of tea at Child's. And here, right besides this typewriter is the couch on which he used to sleep etc. I somehow can't get reconciled to his being dead forever. You see, I am really hurt. First because, as one of my more lovely acquaintances in this country put it, 'I take this sort of thing (meaning death) so seriously' (is not that lovely?), and second because I begin to realize how many of my very best friends are between 60 and 70, i/e/ am up against the problem of 'surviving,' which is the vulgar version of the more serious question: How does one live with the dead? It is obvious, isn't it, that one needs new feelings, new manners, new everything . . . Think of me, sitting in a corner, very quiet, and pondering the problem of 'surviving'.

When Arendt returned from her trip to Europe in the summer of 1951, she went to New Haven to help sort his literary estate. While there, she wrote a poem to mark his passing:

H.B.

Survival.
But how does one live with the dead? Say,
where is the sound of their company,
or the gestures they once made?
We wish that they were still near us.

Who knows the lament that took them away
and drew the veil before their empty gaze?
What helps? That we send ourselves to them,
and turning this feeling around, learn to survive.

In the summer of 1948 Arendt left Schocken Books and took a vacation in Hanover, New Hampshire, to continue working on *The Origins of Totalitarianism*. She had cleared her schedule and cancelled a trip to Europe with the Jewish Cultural Reconstruction Commission to finish the manuscript. While she was there her mother Martha sent word that she had decided to move to England to live with her stepdaughter Eva Beerwald. Arendt's other stepsister, Clara, had committed suicide in April of 1932, suffering from severe mental health problems. And while Arendt had never formed a friendship with either stepsister, Martha had maintained a relationship with Eva over the years. Tensions at home had grown between Martha and Heinrich, with whom Martha never really got along. Her petit-bourgeois sensibility clashed with his working-class ego, and they had been living on top of one another for seven years. Arendt returned to New York for a week to help her mother pack for the move. She saw her off on the *Queen Mary*, and when Arendt returned

Hannah Arendt's mother, Martha.

to New Hampshire she received a telegram from Eva dated 26 July 1948, 7:20 a.m., which read: 'Mother unchanged mistily under drugs awake suffering asthma.' The next day, 27 July, at 7:39 a.m.: 'Mother died sleeping last night arranging cremation.'[14]

Martha had suffered a serious asthma attack on board while crossing the Atlantic and never fully recovered. She was 74 years old.

Martha's passing was not easy for Arendt. She felt that she had mishandled the situation, but she also acknowledged that it had been impossible living together. She wrote to Blücher when she received Eva's telegram: 'Naturally, I'm simultaneously sad and relieved at the same time. It's quite possible that all this was the biggest mistake of my life. I couldn't have simply turned down her request, because it came from a love and a wholeheartedness.'[15] Arendt had wanted to honour her mother's request that she stay as close to her as possible, which she had tried to do for most of her life.

11

Reconciliation

Arendt returned to Europe for the first time in November 1949 as the Executive Director of Jewish Cultural Reconstruction Commission. The Commission had been established by the Conference on Jewish Relations in the spring of 1947 to recover Jewish property looted by the Nazis. In her previous position as Research Director, Arendt wrote a series of 'Tentative Lists of Jewish Cultural Treasures in Axis-Occupied Countries' for *Jewish Social Studies*. The lists were an important political instrument used by the State Department and Allied governments to recognize the Commission as the trusteeship corporation for the reclamation of Jewish property. With the help of others, over the course of several trips to Germany Arendt was able to recover '1,500,000 books of Hebraica and Judaica, countless ritual and artistic objects, and more than 1,000 scrolls of law'.[1]

Arendt worked out of the Commission's headquarters in Wiesbaden. As she travelled across the country by train between Frankfurt, Würzburg, Nuremberg, Erlangen and Heidelberg, she found the towns she once knew in ruins: 'The sight of Germany's destroyed cities and the knowledge of German concentration and extermination camps have covered Europe with a cloud of melancholy.' In a letter to Blücher Arendt ironically compared the German landscape to the ruins of Heidelberg Castle – swept clean and awaiting tourists.

The landscape had changed, but Arendt was able to meet with familiar friends during her trip that she hadn't seen since she was forced to flee, including Alexandre Koyré and Anne Weil (née Mendelssohn) in Paris, her stepsister Eva Beerwald and cousin Else Aron Braude in London, and Karl and Gertrud Jaspers. After the war Jaspers and his wife emigrated to Basel, Switzerland, and Arendt made the time to visit them twice on her trip. Her meetings with Jaspers refreshed and nourished her amidst the chaos of her travel intinerary. She was happy to find him youthful and in good spirits, ready to take on anything, and they spent hours on end talking about philosophy, publishing, Franz Kafka, Heinrich Blücher and Martin Heidegger.

Heidegger and Jaspers had resumed their correspondence after the war, which Jaspers shared with Arendt. Jaspers and Heidegger had a long and complicated relationship that revolved around their philosophical conversations, and continued on and off over the years. Jaspers's trust prompted Arendt to tell him about her relationship with Heidegger before the war, to which he responded, 'Oh, how very exciting.' Jaspers's forthright response relieved and delighted Arendt. But just as Jaspers was unfazed by news of Arendt's relationship with Heidegger, he was troubled by Heidegger's refusal to admit his failures and apologize for joining the Nazi Party. Jaspers could not understand such a failure of moral character. He called Heidegger 'my spiritual enemy'.

Arendt shared Jaspers's reticence and suspected that Heidegger's correspondence with him was disingenuous. Heidegger had treated Jaspers with the same coldness as Edmund Husserl during the war years in his position as Rector of Freiburg University. Barred from holding a teaching position, his name in ruins, Arendt suspected Heidegger of trying to make good to redeem his own reputation. She was unimpressed by Heidegger's letters to Jaspers, and she was ambivalent about seeing Heidegger on her trip. After her meeting with Jaspers she writes to Blücher:

Whether or not I'm going to see Heidegger, I don't know yet – I'll leave everything up to fate. His letters to Jaspers, the ones Jaspers showed me, just as they used to be: the same mix of genuineness and mendacity, or better still cowardice, in which both qualities are primary. With Jaspers I lost a little of my keenness for Heidegger. It always comes back to the same thing: the principle by which relationships are entered into.[2]

Arendt decided to see Heidegger at the last moment, after she was scheduled to give a lecture in Freiburg. On 7 February she sent a letter to him asking if he wanted to meet. There are conflicting narratives about what happened next. As she recounts the meeting to Hilde Fränkel in a letter, Arendt sent Heidegger a simple handwritten note on her hotel stationery, inviting him to visit. He came immediately, and recited 'a sort of tragedy'. In another version, told by Hans Jonas:

After her lecture in Freiburg, there was a knock at her hotel door. Heidegger stood there and said: 'I came to turn myself in.' However, as she told me frankly, the two of them were so overwhelmed by their feelings that I doubt that the discussion came to anything. Her good Heinrich [Blücher] had to take it in stride, for she did not conceal it from him – especially since he himself made liberal use of the freedom of modern marriage. He could be certain of her love, but her renewed relationship with Heidegger now played a part in their life again.[3]

Elzbieta Ettinger, in her book on Arendt and Heidegger, assembles a questionable timeline from their correspondence, in which Heidegger goes to the hotel and takes Arendt back to his house:

During 'that evening,' which Arendt spent alone with Heidegger in his house, the unread letter in her handbag, she was unaware that Heidegger had confessed his infidelity to his wife. Arendt learned about it late at night, when 'half asleep' she read his note in the taxicab on her way back to the hotel.[4]

The day after their reunion, Arendt recounts the evening in a letter to Blücher:

> I went to Freiburg, and Heidegger soon appeared at the hotel. The two of us had a real talk, I think, for the first time in our lives . . . On top of everything, this morning I had an argument with his wife. For twenty-five years now, or from the time she somehow wormed the truth about us out of him, she has clearly made his life a hell on earth. And he, who always, at every opportunity, has been such a notorious liar, evidently (as was obvious from the aggravating conversation the three of us had) never, in all those twenty-five years, refuted that I had been the passion of his life. His wife, I'm afraid, for as long as I'm alive, is ready to drown any Jew in sight. Unfortunately, she is absolutely horrendous.

The exact timeline of events is unclear. As is the case with private relationships, one can never really know what passes between two people. It is evident from the letters, however, that Heidegger was too impatient to wait for the post office to open the next day when he received Arendt's letter, so he wrote a response, put it in an envelope and went to Arendt's hotel to hand deliver his reply. He arrived after 6:30 p.m. and asked for Arendt. A waiter walked him into the dining room and announced his name. When she saw him 'it was as if time suddenly stood still'.[5] From the letters dated 8 and 9 February it appears they spent two evenings together, one without his wife Elfriede, and one with her. It seems possible from their letters that they spent 7 February at the hotel, and then Heidegger drove her to his home in Zähringen, where he had arranged a lunch with Elfriede at noon, but we cannot know for sure.

What is clear from their reunion is that the intimacy between them had not been lost. Heidegger felt a burden lift from his shoulders when they met: 'The morning light has now taken away something dark that hung over our early encounter and over our long-distance waiting.' The darkness refers to the secrecy of their relationship. In his hand-delivered note, which Arendt had not read, he had confessed to her that Elfriede knew about their relationship, and he had arranged a lunch for them the following afternoon to clear the air. For Arendt, their night and morning together were 'confirmation of an entire life'.[6]

Much has been written about Arendt's relationship with Heidegger before and after the war. Whole books have been dedicated to the subject. In *The Human Condition* Arendt writes about the *inter-esse*, the goings on between people in the world. What was between Arendt and Heidegger will remain a topic of speculation, but perhaps two concepts in Arendt's work lend assistance to understanding their relationship. The first is forgiveness and the second is reconciliation. For Arendt, forgiveness was a personal matter: 'Forgiving and the relationship it establishes is always an eminently personal (though not necessarily individual or private) affair in which what was done is forgiven for the sake of who did it.' Love relationships are not political relationships, and in this way, for Arendt, love is unworldly. Through loving and forgiving the other, one can look past *what* they are, with all of their 'qualities and shortcomings . . . achievements, failings, and transgressions', to see with clarity of vision *who* they are. It is for the sake of who a person is that an act can be forgiven, so that an entire life is not reduced to one deed. Whereas forgiveness is personal and deals with the messiness of human emotions, reconciliation rests on reason, and requires equanimity and judgement.

Shortly after Arendt returned from her trip to Europe she began keeping her thinking journals. In a lengthy entry from 1950 she writes about *Verzeihung*, forgiveness, and *Versöhnung*, reconciliation. In the entry, Arendt explores how forgiveness destroys the equality of human relationships by creating a hierarchy between the person who forgives and the person who is forgiven. The act of forgiveness ruins relationships because the person who forgives positions themselves above the person who seeks forgiveness, and the person who seeks forgiveness seeks something another person cannot give. Reconciliation is an alternative to forgiveness. Instead of performing the act of forgiveness, a new beginning is made possible.

Arendt softens the distinction she initially draws between forgiveness and reconciliation in her thinking journals in her discussion of forgiveness, revenge and reconciliation in *The Human Condition*. What they come to share in common is the fundamental quality of new beginnings, which exist infinitely in the world and are initiated every time someone acts.

Arendt's discussion of forgiveness and reconciliation is folded between meditations on love. As much as she enjoyed travelling and reuniting with old friends, Arendt's relationship with Blücher suffered during the three months she was away. He did not keep up with his end of the correspondence, and her letters imploring him to write to her fell on deaf ears:

I am very upset. I simply can't understand your complete lack of sense about the most primitive human responsibilities and obligations. I cannot believe that you have so little imagination that you can't imagine how I feel, careering about the world like a car wheel that has come off, without a single connection to home or to anything I can rely on.[7]

Arendt's frustration was caused in part by Blücher's recent affair, which had come to light shortly before she left. And while monogamy was never a part of their marriage agreement, Arendt felt betrayed by the public manner of Blücher's indiscretion. She had learned about the affair from a common friend, which violated her sense of privacy. Blücher knew about Arendt's relationship with Martin Heidegger and was not jealous. He writes reassuringly to Arendt, 'Let them be jealous that there waits here at home for you your not at all jealous [husband], who, instead of being jealous, really loves you after his fashion.' Ultimately, for Arendt and Blücher fidelity was not the cornerstone of being together. Their acceptance of one another and lack of secrecy gave them a common foundation. Arendt responds to Blücher's letter affirming their love:

> Our hearts have really grown towards each other and our steps go in unison. And this unison cannot be disturbed, even though life goes on. These fools who think themselves loyal if they give up their active lives and bind themselves together into an exclusive One; they then have not only no common life but generally no life at all. If it weren't so risky, one should one day tell the world what marriage really is.

Arendt's understanding of marriage echoes Rainer Maria Rilke's idea of love, where one stands guard over the solitude of another. Arendt and Blücher's marriage embodied the spirit of their work; it was communicative and free, creating necessary space for thinking while always preserving the possibility of the new.

Love, like friendship, belongs to the private realm of human affairs, away from the light of public life. It requires freedom, an ability to move between the different spheres of life, and a commitment to privacy. Arendt insisted on this distinction between private and public, because she believed that when we lose the ability to distinguish between private and public life, freedom is restricted, and when freedom is restricted, movement is no longer possible. And when one is isolated in their thinking and ability to move freely through the world, then it is a warning sign that totalitarianism is encroaching.

12

The Origins of Totalitarianism

Hannah Arendt published *The Origins of Totalitarianism* in 1951, the same year she received American citizenship. After eighteen years, she finally escaped 'the infinitely complex red-tape existence of a stateless person'.[1] When she appeared for her naturalization ceremony she officially changed her name from Johanna Blücher to Hannah Arendt Blücher, marking a new beginning.

Arendt had begun working on *The Origins of Totalitarianism* in 1941 and finished it in 1949, shortly before she travelled to Europe. *Origins* is an epic work that stretches nearly six hundred pages, offering an account of the phenomenal appearance of totalitarianism in the twentieth century. When she began working on *Origins*, Hitler was dead but Stalin was alive, and because Arendt was writing in the moment, the shape of the manuscript changed over time, as new information became available about what had happened in Europe, and what was happening in the Soviet Union.

In the late autumn and early winter of 1944/5 Arendt submitted the first outline of *Origins*, provisionally titled *The Elements of Shame: Anti-Semitism – Imperialism – Racism*, to Mary Underwood, an editor at Houghton Mifflin. Her secondary, provisional title shifted to *The Three Pillars of Hell*, and suggested thirteen chapters under four headings: 'The Jewish Road to the Storm-center of Politics', 'The Disintegration of the National State', 'Expansion and Race' and 'Full-fledged Imperialism'.

Reading across the history of anti-Semitism, Arendt wanted to look at how modern anti-Semitism was bound to imperialism and racism. In 1944 she published an essay titled 'Opinion or Ideology' as the first section of her article 'Race-thinking before Racism' in the *Review of Politics*.[2] This was to become the chapter in *Origins* in which Arendt makes a historical argument about the role 'race-thinking' played in the rise of the Third Reich. According to her analysis, there was a moment in time when race-thinking still belonged to a realm of opinion, but something changed during the Age of Imperialism and the so-called 'Scramble for Africa' at the turn of the century. Race-thinking became an ideology and was weaponized by the state as an instrument of political violence used to expropriate land, resources and labour. Race-thinking was transformed into racism and became an ideology. And it became such a dominant ideology that the public adopted racist opinions without thinking about them. For Arendt, the two dominant ideologies that won over modern mass society were classism and racism. She writes, 'For an ideology differs from a simple opinion in that it claims to possess either the key to history, or the solution for all the "riddles of the universe", or the intimate knowledge of the hidden universal laws which are supposed to rule nature and man.' For Arendt, ideology is not opinion. Whereas race-thinking might have once been an opinion it is now an ideology, and has taken up root in the form of popular prejudice. Which is to say, it cannot be an opinion, because it cannot be freely held.

This analysis remained in *Origins*, and the scope of Arendt's study widened. As news emerged from Europe about the Nazi concentration camps, Arendt began to focus her argument on what made totalitarianism a radically new form of government. She followed the Nuremberg trials and read memoirs of survivors alongside anti-Semitic material. She argued that totalitarianism was distinct from authoritarianism, tyranny and fascism, and rested on the radical atomization of the individual, elimination of spontaneity and political freedom. The defining element of totalitarianism was the instrumentalization of terror and construction of concentration camps. 'The real horror of the concentration and extermination camps,' Arendt writes, 'lies in the fact that the inmates, even if they happen to keep alive, are more effectively cut off from the world of the living than if they had died, because terror enforces oblivion.'[3]

By February 1948 *Origins* had taken shape and Arendt wrote to Houghton Mifflin telling them that the book was in three parts, 'Antisemitism', 'Imperialism' and 'Nazism', and that she was just beginning to write the third part on Nazism as a form of racist, totalitarian regime. But then, as news of Stalinist tactics emerged and Arendt began to read through materials from the Soviet Union, including Zoe Zajdlerowa's memoir *The Dark Side of the Moon*, she decided to revise the last section. *The Origins of Totalitarianism* was published in 1951 with the third section renamed 'Totalitarianism': what information she had learned about Stalin's schema made it apparent that Stalinism was a more fully developed version of totalitarianism than Nazism.

Arendt's *Origins* was the first extensive account of the rise of Hitlerism and Stalinism. It was published on the heels of McCarthyism in America. The American and European right read the book as a testament against the dangers of communism and totalitarianism, and the American and European left criticized Arendt for collapsing Marxism with Stalinism, arguing that Stalinism was a perversion of Marxism. Other critiques came from scholars in the social sciences, such as Eric Voegelin, a German-American political scientist. In 1953 Voegelin published a short review of *Origins* in the *Review of Politics*, which led to a brief exchange. Arendt and Voegelin agreed on several points, but Arendt's chief quarrel was 'with the present state of the historical and political sciences and their growing incapacity for making distinctions'. Terms like nationalism, imperialism and totalitarianism were 'used indiscriminately for all kinds of political phenomena'.[4]

Arendt and Voegelin had different views of what constituted political understanding. For Arendt, all thinking moves from experience, which means that the facts of events are essential to understanding, whereas Voegelin insisted that historical events could only be understood by approaching them through essential political principles removed from experience. What Voegelin and others did not understand was Arendt's methodology in writing, which rejected essentialism and historicism. In a reply to Voegelin, Arendt outlines her approach:

My first problem was how to write historically about something – totalitarianism – which I did not want to conserve but on the contrary felt engaged to destroy. My way of solving this problem has given rise to the reproach that the book was lacking in unity. What I did – and what I might have done anyway because of my previous training and the way of my thinking – was to discover the chief elements of totalitarianism and to analyze them in historical terms, tracing these elements back in history as far as I deemed proper and necessary. That is, I did not write a history of totalitarianism but an analysis in terms of history; I did not write a history of anti-Semitism or of imperialism, but analyzed the element of Jew-hatred and the element of expansion insofar as these elements were still clearly visible and played a decisive role in the totalitarian phenomenon itself. The book, therefore, does not really deal with the 'origins' of totalitarianism – as its title unfortunately claims – but gives a historical account of the elements which crystallized into totalitarianism; this account is followed by an analysis of the elemental structure of totalitarian movements and domination itself. The elementary structure of totalitarianism is the hidden structure of the book while its more apparent unity is provided by certain fundamental concepts which run like red threads through the whole.[5]

The language of 'elements' and 'crystallization' comes from Walter Benjamin's work on historical materialism in *Theses on the Philosophy of History*, which rejects the linear temporality of historicism. By looking at the various elements Arendt was able to illustrate how they had crystallized together in the phenomenal appearance of totalitarianism, and how they persisted in the world even after the dissolution of Hitler's and Stalin's regimes.

At the heart of *Origins* is the chapter on 'The Political Emancipation of the Bourgeoisie' in the second section on 'Imperialism'. There Arendt discusses the collapse between the public and private realms of life, which were preceded by the liberation of private, economic interests into the public, political realm, what today we might call the privatization of politics. Where once businessmen were concerned with their families and private lives, enjoying a life of consumption, they now entered into the public sphere, bringing their business models with them. In this section on 'Imperialism', Arendt details how private business interests increasingly took over the functions of the state, because they needed new markets in order that they could continue to grow: 'Businessmen became politicians and were acclaimed as statesmen, while statesmen were taken seriously only if they talked the language of successful businessmen.'[6] In order to reach new markets they needed the support of the government to step outside the nation-state borders. As a result, businessmen slowly replaced politicians and matters of private economy became matters of the state. But the principle of unfettered growth that drove private interests was incompatible with the need for stable political institutions. Arendt turns to Thomas Hobbes as a theorist of power to think about the principle of expansion for expansion's sake, which elevates private economic interests to the level of politics. Ultimately this leads to the socialization of the private and public realms, levelling class difference, while destroying stable political institutions by doing away with the public sphere.

For Arendt this meant that totalitarianism makes political action impossible because it destroys the possibility for spontaneous action between people.

If the power to act comes from 'acting in concert', that is with one another, then isolated individuals are powerless by definition. Totalitarian government rules by terror, isolating people from one another, while turning each individual in his or her lonely isolation against all others. The world becomes a wilderness, as Arendt describes it, where neither experience nor thought are possible. One way totalitarianism turns people into isolated, lonely individuals is through the systematic blurring of reality and fiction. And this blurring relies upon the inability to see or think discerningly when people are confronted with ideologies that rely upon spreading fear:

> Just as terror, even in its pre-total, merely tyrannical form ruins all relationships between men, so the self-compulsion of ideological thinking ruins all relationship with reality. The preparation has succeeded when people have contact with their fellow men as well as the reality around them; for together with these contacts, men lose the capacity of both experience and thought. The ideal subject of totalitarian rule is not the convinced Nazi or the convinced Communist, but people for whom the distinction between fact and fiction (*i.e.*, the reality of experience) and the distinction between true and false (*i.e.*, the standards of thought) no longer exist.

Drawing from Martin Luther, Arendt highlights how loneliness leads one down thought paths to the worst possible outcomes, following chains of logic that are not rooted in reality, but the imagination. She writes, 'Under the conditions of loneliness, therefore, the self-evident is no longer just a means of the intellect and begins to be productive, to develop its own lines of "thought".' The notorious extremism of totalitarian movements, far from having anything to do with true radicalism, consists indeed in this 'thinking everything to the worst', in this deducing process which always arrives at the worst possible conclusions.

The loss of meaning in the modern world is characterized by the underlying conditions of homelessness, rootlessness and loneliness. In the final pages of *Origins* Arendt identifies loneliness as the underlying cause of all totalitarian movements. Loneliness, she writes, is the common ground of terror. Whereas isolation 'concerns only the political realm of life, loneliness concerns human life as a whole'. Tyranny destroys the public realm of life by isolating individuals and destroying their capacity for political action, but totalitarianism also insists on destroying private life as well. Totalitarianism 'bases itself on loneliness, on the experience of not belonging to the world at all, which is among the most radical and desperate experiences of man'.

The German word Arendt uses for loneliness is *verlassenheit*, which means a state of being abandoned, or abandon-ness. In this loneliness, one is unable to realize one's full capacity for action as a human being, and one is unable to make new beginnings. Totalitarianism destroys the space between people by ruining their ability to think, and their relationships with themselves. One becomes isolated in one's thought, unable to tell the difference between what is real and what is not. And in this, loneliness is dangerous because it destroys the space of solitude, which is a necessary condition for thinking.

Shortly after the publication of *Origins*, Arendt accepted a position as a Visiting Professor at Princeton University, where she was the first female faculty hire. The following year, with a grant from the Guggenheim Foundation, she began working on her second book, intended to be called *Totalitarian Elements of Marxism*, which was framed as a follow-up to *The Origins of Totalitarianism*. She thought the most serious gap in *Origins* was the lack of conceptual analysis around Bolshevism, and she wanted to take a closer look at the ideologies and methods of totalitarian regimes and the legacy of Marxism.[7] With a fellowship from the Foundation, Arendt spent March to August 1952 in Europe, conducting research in various libraries, while visiting with her friends Anne Weil and Alfred Kazin. Unofficially she continued working for the Jewish Cultural Reconstruction Commission, lecturing in various cities, and taking time for a holiday in St Moritz with Karl Jaspers and his wife. Unlike her first trip back to Europe, she was able to enjoy the renewed landscape.[8] She was so moved by the beauty of the natural colours and architecture that she wrote a poem to Blücher marvelling at the scenery:

Drive through France

Earth writes poetry field after field,
braiding trees alongside,
letting us weave our way,
around the lands in the world.

Blossoms rejoice in the wind,
Grass shoots out into soft supple beds,
Sky turns blue and greets with lightness,
Sun spins into soft chains.

People go unlost –
Earth, sky, light and woods –
Reborn every spring
Playfully in the play of omnipotence.[9]

When Arendt returned to the United States she began teaching and lecturing on Marx in the middle of the McCarthy trials. The chilling intellectual atmosphere did not temper Arendt's work on Marx, though. At the height of the zealous anti-communist movement, she published an article titled 'The Ex-Communists' in which she drew a distinction between ex-communists who switch ideologies but not ways of being in the world, and former communists who understood one could not separate methods and aims.[10] It was no small feat of courage to publish something so bold at the height of McCarthyism, as the attorney general threatened to investigate and deport 'alien citizens' for being subversive. But Arendt was never one to shy away from controversy, or bow to ideological demands.

It was not until 1956, at the end of the McCarthy era, that the United States government opened a file on Arendt at the behest of a concerned father who thought his daughter was being influenced by her teaching:

> Mr. X advised he felt that HANNAH ARENDT was very dangerous to the best interests of this country in view of the fact she is a professor who travels around the United States instructing at numerous colleges as a visiting professor. He stated his daughter changed her thinking completely after taking courses from HANNAH ARENDT at the University of California, Berkeley, California, in 1955, and feels that it was her influence which had influenced his daughter to go to Europe to study under Professor PAUL RICOEUR.

The FBI determined that the non-specific complaint did not warrant an active investigation.

Arendt received an invitation to give the Christian Gauss seminars on 'Criticism' at Princeton University in autumn 1953, making her the first woman to do so. The faculty and students were delighted to have a female professor for a change, but she was annoyed that she was treated as the 'token woman', as she expressed to Kurt Blumenfeld: 'At the closing ceremony, and ever

Hannah Arendt and Heinrich Blücher, 1950s.

so slightly tipsy, I enlightened these dignified gentlemen about what an exception Jew is, and tried to make clear to them that I have necessarily found myself here an exception woman.' Arendt had no interest in being the 'exception woman', just as she had no interest in being the 'exception Jew'. When Princeton University offered her the rank of full professor a few years later in 1959, she threatened to decline because the *New York Times* stressed the fact that she would be the 'first woman'. Arendt wanted to be acknowledged for her thinking, not for character traits that were mere facts of her existence, and she held firm on this line over the course of her career. When she was interviewed about her appointment, she told an interviewer, 'I am not disturbed at all about being a woman professor, because I am quite used to being a woman.'[11]

In 1952 Heinrich Blücher received an offer to teach at Bard College in upstate New York from its president, James Case. Case had heard about Blücher's teaching at the New School from Horace Kallen in the philosophy department and hired Blücher to create a common course for Bard's freshman class. Case thought Blücher was 'a Socratic man', in part because Blücher's approach to the study of philosophy was old-fashioned. Blücher rejected the turn towards analytical philosophy and had certain ideas about the place of philosophy within the scheme of the social sciences. Blücher, much like Plato's Socrates, thought it was philosophy's responsibility to inspire the human imagination. His first syllabus for the common course included Abraham, Buddha, Lao-Tse, Homer, Heraclitus and Socrates: those 'Arch-fathers of the free personality'.[12] The first year Blücher offered the common course, Hannah Arendt followed along with the readings at home.

13

Amor Mundi

'In 1957, an earth-born object made by man was launched into the universe, where for some weeks it circled the earth according to the same laws of gravitation that swing and keep in motion the celestial bodies – the sun, the moon, and the stars.'[1]

Published in 1958, Hannah Arendt's *The Human Condition* begins with a reflection on man's exploration of space, a year after Sputnik launched. Written on the heels of *The Origins of Totalitarianism*, the Second World War, the use of atomic weapons and with the spectre of the Cold War looming, Arendt's work is fundamentally about the discovery of human freedom, its gradual, fateful disappearance from the world, and the elusiveness of the conditions of its recovery.

Part of what makes *The Human Condition* a great work of the twentieth century is that Arendt is doing many things at once, and the book does not sit comfortably within any disciplinary boundaries. Arendt is not questioning a single political problem, she is not writing political philosophy, and she is not outlining practical solutions for contemporary political problems. Instead she is addressing the fundamental activities of human life and thinking about how they have changed over time.

When the poet W. H. Auden reviewed *The Human Condition* for *Encounter* magazine in 1959, he said he felt as if it had been especially written for him. 'The author seems to have created a world for which I have been waiting all my life; in the case of a "think" book, it seems to answer precisely those questions which I have been putting to myself.' *The Human Condition* is a book to think with, and it is a book that demonstrates the activity of thinking itself.

In the 1950s the spectres of automation and atomic warfare painted a bleak picture of the future. 'At all times in history men have felt anxious about their own fate or the fate of their class or community, but there has seldom been a time, I believe, when the present and future of the whole human endeavor on this earth have seemed questionable to so many people.' Auden suggested that *The Human Condition* be read almost like a dictionary of conceptual definitions: earth, world, labour, work, action, private, social, public, political, promises, forgiveness.

Structurally, the work relies upon an apparatus of conceptual distinctions that focuses on what Arendt identified as the three fundamental activities of the human condition: labour, work and action. Each of these activities corresponds to one of the basic conditions under which life on earth has been given to man. The human condition of labour is life itself and corresponds to the biological processes of the human body. The human condition of work is worldliness and corresponds to the non-naturalness of human existence. It is what is made. And 'Plurality is the condition of human action, because we are all the same, that is, human, in such a way that nobody is ever the same as anyone else who ever lived, lives, or will live.'[2] Labour, work and action, and their corresponding conditions, are 'intimately connected with the underlying conditions of human existence: birth and death, natality and mortality'.

In these distinctions we see the different ways in which Arendt is using the word 'condition'. She is referring to 'the conditions under which life has been given to man', thinking about how we are conditioned by the world around us, and how everything we come into contact with turns immediately into a condition for human existence.[3]

Alongside labour, work and action, Arendt draws a set of spatial distinctions between private, social and public, in order to think about the different realms of life we move between. In German she translated these spaces into *raumen*, or 'rooms'. What is at stake in *The Human Condition* is freedom in the modern era, which requires the ability to move between the different realms of life. The rise of modernity destroyed the ability to distinguish between different forms of human activity and their corresponding realms, which meant that we were no longer free to move between the different realms of life and engage in human activity. Everything was reduced to the social, and every activity became an activity of labour for mere consumption.

Looking at the rise of mass society, and how it transforms all work into labour, Arendt develops a concept she terms 'modern worldly alienation'. Modern worldly alienation is characterized by the twofold flight of man from earth into the universe, and from the world into the self. The socialization of the private and public realms, the rise of consumer society and the loss of the commons, are only possible because of wealth accumulation, in which 'the world and the very worldliness of man are sacrificed'.[4]

In *Origins* Arendt detailed the iron-band of totalitarianism that presses men together, making it impossible to move in the world; in *The Human Condition* she examines how freedom of movement is being lost in the modern world to the rise of the social. The rise of modern mass society diminished the ability to distinguish between public and private life, which led to a loss of common sense and a commonly shared world. Turning to Jean-Jacques Rousseau's *Confessions* (1782) and René Descartes' *Meditations* (1641), Arendt explored how modernity marked man's flight into himself, creating a new kind of individualism. This turn in thinking taught man that he could no longer trust his own sensual experiences in the world. Instead, the world was transformed into a knowable object, quantifiable and replicable. Plurality, the fundamental characteristic of the human condition, is flattened; meaning becomes impossible because there is no shared experience of the world, and remembrance becomes impossible when there are no public spaces for appearance and recognition. This means, Arendt argues, that people no longer strive for greatness or immortality, instead they strive to escape the human condition altogether. But in order to be fully human one must appear in public before others, and one must have a space of privacy for solitude to think. Only in that space of solitude can one transform worldly happenings into inner experience, which becomes 'like a mirror in whose reflection truth might appear'. And part of that truth is that we must inhabit the earth together and build the world in common.

What is at stake in the modern world is freedom and political action. The socialization of the public and private realms means that one loses the ability to distinguish between public and private life, which is necessary for freedom. With the loss of this distinction, one also loses the ability to move freely, because there is nowhere to move to when everything has become the social, or when everything has become the political. Arendt described spaces of freedom as islands that appear in a sea or as oases in a desert.[5]

The Human Condition grew out a series of lectures Arendt gave at the University of Chicago in April 1956, which were material for a study of 'The Totalitarian Elements of Marxism'. *Origins* dealt with philosophical shifts in thinking that preceded the emergence of totalitarianism, and Arendt wanted to look at the qualities in Marx's work that might have contributed to the catastrophe of the twentieth century. But as Arendt read through Marx's writing, she found his work rooted in the tradition of Western philosophy, stretching back to Plato. And for Arendt this meant that one cannot accuse Marx of being the father of totalitarian ideology any more than Plato or Aristotle. It is not that Marx's writing broke the tradition of Western political philosophy and opened up space for totalitarianism; it's that 'One might argue that the thread of our tradition was broken, in the sense that our traditional political categories were never meant for such a situation.'[6]

As Arendt began writing she was in correspondence with Karl Jaspers. Jaspers had just published an essay on Marx and Freud in *Der Monat*, and Arendt read his piece in the context of his earlier work on Von der Wahrheit, which was critical of Marx. Arendt tells Jaspers: 'I would like to try to rescue Marx's honor in your sight. Not that what you say about him isn't right.'[7] Arendt and Jaspers disagreed about justice and freedom. For Jaspers, and Arendt's husband Blücher, Marx's project was not concerned with justice, but rather with freedom from labour. Arendt tried to read Marx in line with Kant, in order to favourably think about his project as being one of creating a just society, but Jaspers challenged Marx's motivation, which he thought was impure and unjust at the root, because he drew 'from the negative with an image of man'. He wrote to Arendt that Marx was 'the hate incarnate of a pseudo-prophet the style of Ezekiel'.[8]

Arendt was more favourable to Marx than Jaspers. Her critique was not a wholesale rejection. Thinking through his work in *Debatten über das Holzdiebstahlsgesetz* (Debates over the Theft of Wood) of 1842, Arendt responds to Jaspers's critique, drawing attention to Marx's discussion of the 'de-humanizing of man' and the 'de-naturing of nature'. She argues that these two elements are at the heart of what Marx meant by abstract society, and that a rebellion against these elements runs throughout his work: 'I do not mean to defend him as a scholar (although he was a great scholar, scholarship is the very thing he destroyed with his ideological overlay) and surely not as a philosopher, but as a rebel and revolutionary.'[9] It would be a mistake to think Arendt was Marxian, however; she wasn't. Arendt had turned to Marx in order to think through what she called the break in tradition, which began with Plato, ran up through Nietzsche, and ended in Marx's inversion of the hierarchy between the *vita activa* and the *vita contemplativa*. In his Eleventh Thesis in the 'Theses on Feuerbach', Marx said: 'The philosophers have only interpreted the world, in various ways; the point is to change it.'

Arendt's central criticism of Marx is that he elevated the labouring activity to the fundamental activity of the human condition. For her, this is summarized in Marx's sentence: 'Labour is the creator of man.' In Arendt's tripartite distinction between labour, work and action, she posits that it is labour which binds us to nature, and our animal condition. For her, the good life cannot come from the labouring activity alone, we must be liberated from labour and free to participate in the public realm, to appear before others in word and deed.

When Hannah Arendt translated *The Human Condition* from English into German, she retitled it *Vita activa oder von tätigen Leben* (The Life of Action or On the Active Life). Arendt argues that the fundamental activities of the *vita activa* have up until now chiefly been considered from the standpoint of the *vita contemplativa*. Arendt is further drawing a distinction between the *vita contemplativa*, as the traditional work of professional thinkers, and the life of the mind, which does not belong to any professional class. Part of Arendt's project is to consider the life of action from the perspective of human experience and activity in the world. In her discussion of the philosopher Thales in *The Life of the Mind* (1977), Arendt notes that when we think about the world from lofty, philosophical heights, we forfeit the common sense necessary for being present in the world. In order to be present, and see what is before us, thinking must move from experience, and not philosophical ideals. At the end of the 'Prologue' Arendt offers an axiom: 'What I propose, therefore, is very simple: it is nothing more than to think what we are doing.'[10] This axiom carries great weight;

it is an indictment against those more concerned with the heavenly bodies than the world at their feet, and it is a plea to pause and consider the position from which we approach thinking about the activities of the human condition.

In an entry in one of her thinking journals, dated August 1955, Arendt wrote: 'Heidegger is wrong: man is not "thrown" "in the world"; if we are thrown, then – no differently from animals – onto the earth. Man is precisely guided, not thrown, precisely for that reason his continuity arises and the way he belongs appears. Poor us, if we are thrown into the world!'[11] Arendt rejected Heidegger's conception of 'thrownness' as a form of despair. Being in the world means being with, and this was precisely the thing Heidegger was incapable of offering so many years before. In certain ways, Arendt's work in *The Human Condition* is a rejection and critique of Heidegger's conception of thinking, a critique that she would return to in her final work.

When the German edition of *The Human Condition* was published in 1960 Arendt had the publisher send Heidegger a copy, with the following note:

> You will see that the book does not contain a dedication. If things had ever worked out properly between us – and I mean between, that is, neither you nor me – I would have asked you if I might dedicate it to you; it came directly out of the first Freiburg days and hence owes practically everything to you in every respect. As things are, I did not think it was possible, but I wanted to at least mention the bare fact to you in one way or another. All the best![12]

In Arendt's papers at the German Literature Archive in Marbach, Germany, there is a handwritten draft of the manuscript, signed 'Hannah', along with a slip of notebook paper containing a dedication:

Re Vita Activa:
The dedication of this book is omitted.
How could I dedicate it to you,
trusted one,
whom I was faithful
and not faithful to,
And both with love.

Arendt did not send the dedication, and there is no record of Heidegger responding to her book, though it appears from her thinking journals that it was the subject of at least one conversation.

When Arendt was finishing *The Human Condition* in 1955, she wrote to Jaspers saying that she would like to dedicate *The Human Condition* in his honour: 'I've begun so late, really only in recent years, to truly love the world that I shall be able to do that now. Out of gratitude, I want to call my book on political theory "Amor Mundi".' This passage comes in the middle of her letter to Jaspers, where Arendt is describing the 'melancholy task' she's been working on – writing introductions for books by two deceased friends, Hermann Broch and Waldemar Gurian. Within this statement there is a recognition of and reckoning with the events of the past. What does it mean to love the world in the face of such great loss? In Arendt's lecture notes for a course she taught on the 'History of Political Theory', she offers one answer: 'The political writer loves the world, the world of the *pragmata ton athropon* (the world of human affairs) . . .'

Love of the world is about understanding and reconciling one's self with the world as it is. Or, in Arendt's own words, it is the idea that we must 'face and come to terms with what really happened'. For Arendt, *Amor Mundi* is bound up with her axiom at the beginning of *The Human Condition* that we must stop and think what we are doing. There is a form of self-reflective thinking contained within these ideas, since in order to see the world as it is one must stand on the sidelines, find perspective and a place of solitude for thinking. Loving the world requires reckoning with the world, which for Arendt means that we need to find some distance from our experiences in order to tell a story about them.

14

Between Past and Future

When Hannah Arendt finished *The Human Condition*, she began working on an 'Introduction to Politics'. In her application to the Rockefeller Foundation, she describes the work as an excavation of political concepts:

> In terms of human activities, it will be concerned exclusively with action and thought. The purpose of the book is twofold: First, a critical examination of the chief traditional concepts and conceptual frameworks of political thinking – such as means and ends, authority, government, power, law, war, etc. By criticism I do not mean 'debunking'. I shall try to find out where these concepts came from before they become like worn-out coins and abstract generalizations. I therefore shall examine the concrete historical and generally political experiences which gave rise to political concepts. For the experiences behind even the most worn-out concepts remain valid and must be recaptured and reactualized if one wishes to escape certain generalizations that have proved pernicious.[1]

'Introduction to Politics' became *Between Past and Future*: *Eight Exercises in Political Thought*. It was first published in 1961 as *Six Exercises in Political Thought*, and then expanded to eight in the second edition in 1968 to include 'Truth and Politics' and an essay on 'The Conquest of Space and the Stature of Man'. The 'exercises' in *Between Past and Future* offer an 'experience of *how* to think; they do not contain prescriptions of what to think or which truths to hold'.

Between Past and Future occupies an unique space in Arendt's work, because it illustrates her understanding of thinking, while addressing one of the central claims that underpins her work: 'the break in tradition'. Arendt takes on what it means to think without the concepts and categories provided by tradition, history and authority. With the break in tradition caused by the appearance of totalitarianism in the twentieth century, Arendt was free to look to the past for what might be salvaged, but she was not beholden to it. She was free to think the world anew. To repeat the words of the French poet and resistance fighter René Char: 'Our inheritance was left to us by no testament.'

Arendt turns to Franz Kafka's parable 'He' in order to give language to this way of thinking and judging, arguing that 'He' picks up where Char's aphorism leaves off, and offers an 'exact description of this predicament'.[2] In the parable Kafka describes the mental phenomenon of a thought-event. 'He' stands on a battleground, caught between forces of past and future – the past pressing him forward, the future pressing him back. But time is not a continuum, it is broken where 'He' stands. It is the insertion of man into the world that breaks up the endless and indifferent flow of ordinary time. It is his appearance that contains the possibility of the new. In the parable, 'He' is caught between the past and future that condition 'his' existence. Arendt draws a parallelogram of forces that chart a plane of movement, jumping out of the 'fighting line' of experience.

Kafka's 'He' is 'the old dream Western metaphysics has dreamed from Parmenides to Hegel of a timeless, spaceless, suprasensuous realm'. In order to dismantle this dream, Arendt reworks Kafka's parable and situates 'He' within the realm of worldly affairs: 'The trouble with Kafka's metaphor is that by jumping out of the fighting line "He" jumps out of this world altogether and judges from outside though not necessarily from above.' The battleground for Kafka's 'He' is man's home on earth; in Arendt's reading the physical battleground gives way to the metaphysical battleground for being itself. Arendt is using Kafka to address the metaphysical fallacy that conflates being with meaning.

Thinking must move from experience in order to bear upon the world of experience, otherwise it risks lapsing into metaphysical speculation. Arendt writes, '[thinking] arises out of the incidents of lived experience and must remain bound to them as the only guideposts by which to take its bearings'.[3] It is only from such thinking that one has the ability to give meaning to their experiences through the act of storytelling. Arendt describes thinking as the two-in-one conversation that one has with oneself, it is a dialogic activity. And in thinking the self-consciousness is able to address the conscience, one is able to imagine the world from the perspective of another, and one is able to give meaning to one's life.

In the autumn of 1959 Hannah Arendt travelled to Hamburg to accept the Lessing Prize, flew to Berlin to settle her restitution claims, spent a week on holiday in Florence with Mary McCarthy, visited Anne Weil in Brussels and stayed with Karl and Gertrud Jaspers in Basel for a week at the end of October. When Arendt returned home, she and Heinrich Blücher moved from Morningside Heights to apartment 12A at 370 Riverside Drive. In a letter to Gertrud Jaspers, Arendt describes their new home:

Two studies with a fantastically beautiful view of the river. Completely quiet, no noise from either the street or the neighbors. Four large, nicely proportioned rooms and a small room. Very nice kitchen and pantry, generous closets, huge ones, some of which you can walk right into. The building very well kept up and with a doorman day and night.[4]

Arendt writes to Jaspers, 'The doorman is a kind of private policeman that one has to pay for here now because the city police can't cope with juvenile delinquency anymore.'[5] The tenor of Arendt's letter is marked by her observations about the racial tensions in America:

> the high schools in New York gave all the students of the senior classes the assignment of thinking up an appropriate punishment for Hitler. A Negro girl wrote: He should have black skin put on him and be forced to live in the United States. The girl won first prize and a four-year scholarship to college![6]

The story was testament to how bad race relations were in the United States, and Arendt's anecdote was prompted by a reflection on an award she had just received from the Longview Foundation for her essay 'Reflections on Little Rock', which had been published a year earlier in *Dissent* magazine.

'Reflections on Little Rock' remains one of Arendt's most contentious essays. It was originally written in 1957 for *Commentary* magazine when Arendt saw a photograph of the fifteen-year-old black student Elizabeth Eckford as she tried to enter Little Rock Central High School surrounded by a hostile mob of white students and the Arkansas National Guard. The image was shocking, and Arendt's point of enquiry was: 'what would I do if I were a Negro mother?' Instead of affirming the need for segregation, Arendt saw schoolchildren being mobilized for political battle.

Her piece was delayed because of the controversial nature of her reflections. After several months, the editors at *Commentary* offered to include the piece alongside a response by the American philosopher Sidney Hook, but Arendt decided to withdraw the essay from *Commentary* altogether. Hook's response, 'Democracy and Desegregation', was printed in the *New Leader* on 21 April 1958, a year before Arendt's essay was published in *Dissent*. Arendt allowed

Dissent to feature the essay, with some preliminary corrections and remarks alongside two critical replies, because she wanted to disrupt what she saw as 'the repetition of liberal clichés' in which the discussion of these issues was being held.[7]

In 'Reflections' Arendt critiques the Supreme Court decision in *Brown v. The Board of Education*, which overturned *Plessy v. Ferguson* and the doctrine of 'separate but equal', thereby forcing integration. Arendt's argument relied upon her distinction between the social and the political that she outlined in *The Human Condition*. Political change must come through persuasion, not force. But Arendt's understanding of persuasion was not the liberal understanding of persuasion, and it would be a misreading to make this argument. She was not a progressive or a liberal – her understanding of persuasion was rooted in Jaspers's philosophy and Kant's *Critique of Judgement*. This form of persuasion is a way of remaining open to language and the radical possibility of otherness. One is not only *free* to imagine the world from the perspective of another, they have an ethical obligation to so.

In the *Brown v. Board* decision, Arendt saw proponents of segregation using the federal government to circumvent the necessity of political battle, and she was critical of parents using their children for political gains; educational institutions are social spaces, which should be left untouched by politics. In her opinion, the government should not interfere with schooling and cannot enforce social equality, which is distinct from political equality. In her view, social equality must be won from the bottom up, through conversation not legislation.

Among the responses was an interview given by the writer Ralph Ellison, printed in Robert Penn Warren's collection *Who Speaks for the Negro?* (2014). Discussing the '*ideal*' of sacrifice', Ellison says:

Hannah Arendt's failure to grasp the importance of this ideal among Southern Negroes caused her to fly way off into left field in her 'Reflections on Little Rock,' in which she charged Negro parents with exploiting their children during the struggle to integrate the schools. But she has absolutely no conception of what goes on in the minds of Negro parents when they send their kids through those lines of hostile people . . . in the outlook of many of these parents (who wish that the problem didn't exist), the child is expected to face the terror and contain his fear and anger precisely because he is a Negro American.[8]

Arendt responded to Ellison's review in a private letter:

You are entirely right: it is precisely this 'ideal of sacrifice' which I didn't understand; and since my starting point was a consideration of the situation of Negro kids in forcibly integrated schools, this failure to understand caused me indeed to go into an entirely wrong direction . . . Your remarks seem to me entirely right, that I now see that I simply did not understand the complexities of the situation.[9]

Ellison did not change Arendt's thinking about the political and constitutional issues at stake, but he did convince her that she had overlooked an important psychological aspect in considering her point of departure.

Many scholars have addressed Hannah Arendt's writings on race. Some view her Little Rock essay as an anomaly in her work, others view it as a contradiction in her thinking between the condition of plurality and the right to discrimination. Some contend that she was blind to the social significance of racism in the United States. Those who argue that Arendt was prejudiced turn to her use of philosophical concepts like Kantian judgement and the idea of an 'enlarged mentality' (the ability to imagine the world from the perspective of another) to demonstrate a kind of epistemic failure. Those who have tried to rescue Arendt's work on Little Rock have turned primarily to two arguments: the first is that Arendt's concern was with the welfare of the children. She did not think children should be used for political battles, whether it was protesting against the Vietnam War or fighting for racial integration. The second argument is that Arendt was wary of centralized government, and did not think it was possible to legislate racism from the hearts of men.

For Arendt, the rhetoric of equality is dangerous to democratic political life, and she consistently argued that men would only ever be equal in the sense that they were unequal. She wagered that even if social, economic and educational equality were achieved in the United States, it would increase discrimination against black people. For her, this line of reasoning was not inconsistent with the political argument that 'the right to free association, and therefore to discrimination, has greater validity that the principle of equality.' In dismissing equality from politics, Arendt saw no distinction in the plight of oppressed peoples who were excluded from the realm of public appearances. And in doing so, one might argue, she overlooked the particular conditions of oppression to argue in favour of a universal good, one that is founded on discrimination.

Arendt's essay was consistent with her other writings on race, and the cost of writing such a piece was controversy, to which she was not a stranger.

15

Eichmann in Jerusalem

When Hannah Arendt published *Eichmann in Jerusalem: A Report on the Banality of Evil* in 1963, Irving Howe and Lionel Abel summoned a meeting of New York's literary society. The forum was hosted by *Dissent* magazine in the dodgy Hotel Diplomat in Downtown Manhattan and, in the words of the poet Robert Lowell, 'the meeting was like a trial, the stoning of an outcast member of the family'. It was nothing short of a war room. Hundreds of people crowded into a hall as the historian Raul Hilberg, Zionist author Marie Syrkin and Harvard professor Daniel Bell approached the podium to prosecute Arendt *in absentia*. Arendt was invited to attend, but she was away teaching in Chicago. Each time her name was mentioned, it 'was greeted with derisive clapping' and 'savage sighs of amazement'. Abel furiously pounded the table arguing that Arendt had claimed the Holocaust was banal, that she found Nazis more sympathetic than their victims and, that she was blaming the Jewish people for their own suffering. Her one defender was Alfred Kazin, who walked self-consciously to the podium and said, 'After all, Hannah didn't kill any Jews.' He was laughed off stage.[1] Mary McCarthy said, the event 'assumed the proportions of a pogrom'.

Arendt was on holiday in the Catskills in the summer of 1960 when the news broke that Adolf Eichmann had been captured in Argentina by Mossad agents of the Israeli government. She saw his arrest as an opportunity to 'confront the realm of human affairs and human deeds'. She wrote to the editor of the *New Yorker*, William Shawn, and proposed that she cover the trial. It was her 'last opportunity to see a chief Nazi in the flesh' and she wanted to expose herself to the 'evildoer'.[2]

As the trial was set to begin in the spring of 1961, Arendt rearranged her chaotic teaching schedule between Northwestern, Columbia and Vassar universities, and postponed a one-year grant from the Rockefeller Foundation. She told the Foundation: 'You will understand I think why I should cover this trial; I missed the Nuremberg trials, I never saw these people in the flesh, and this is probably my only chance.' She wrote to Vassar: 'To attend this trial is somehow, I feel, an obligation I owe my past.'[3]

Arendt flew to Israel by way of Paris on 7 April 1961. She was joined by Chanan Klenbort, who met her at the airport with his family, along with her old friend Kurt Blumenfeld, who was living in Israel, and her second cousin Edna Fürst. Arendt had not been back to Israel since she sailed there with Youth Aliyah in 1935 and was happy to arrive. She describes her flight across the Mont Blanc massif, along the Italian coast and over Crete as 'enchanting'. The trial was scheduled to begin on 11 April, and when Arendt arrived the media was in a frenzy, fearful that the trial would fall behind schedule. She immediately postponed her return trip so she could stay a week longer, with trips to visit friends scheduled in-between attending the trial. She had reserved a room at the Hotel Moriyah on King George Street in the centre of the city, but it proved too loud, so she relocated to the Hotel-Pension Reich in Beit Hakerem.

In a letter to Heinrich Blücher on 20 April Arendt offers her initial impressions of the trial:

> Here everything is going as expected, ups and downs, with
> the ghost in the glass cage listening to his voice sounding
> from the magnetic tape. I imagine you've read that he
> would like publicly to hang himself. I was speechless. The

Hannah Arendt in Jerusalem, 1961.

whole thing is so damned banal and indescribably low and
repulsive. I don't understand it yet, but it seems to me that
the penny will drop at some point, probably in my lap.[4]

From the beginning, Arendt was frustrated by the proceedings.
She expected a trial, to witness a case built against Eichmann for
the atrocities that he committed. Instead she was confronted with a
clown in a glass case and a display of 'cheap theatrics'.[5] Eichmann's
name wasn't mentioned for days on end, and instead of trying
the evildoer himself, the proceedings were turned into 'a kind of
historical stock-taking' for 'the sorrows of the Jewish people'. She
was eager to get away, and at the same time she was afraid she
would miss something if she left. [6]

When the trial ended on 15 December 1961 Adolf Eichmann was
found guilty of 'crimes against the Jewish people' and sentenced
to death. On 1 June 1962, after his appeal was denied by the
Israeli appellate court, he was hanged. Arendt's reportage on the
trial appeared in a five-part series for the *New Yorker* between 15
February and 16 March 1963. The book form version, *Eichmann in
Jerusalem: A Report on a Banality of Evil*, was published in May.

At the end of *Eichmann in Jerusalem* Hannah Arendt rejects the
court's judgement and sentencing of Eichmann and proposes her
own:

For politics is not like the nursery; in politics obedience
and support are the same. And just as you supported and
carried out a policy of not wanting to share the earth with
the Jewish people and the people of a number of other
nations – as though you and your superiors had any right
to determine who should and who should not inhabit the
world – we find that no one, that is, no member of the human
race, can be expected to want to share the earth with you.
This is the reason, and the only reason, you must hang.[7]

She frames the question of war crimes outside the law as a matter of sharing the world in common with one's fellow human beings. Eichmann had to die because his actions could not be reconciled with the world we must share in common. He violated the fundamental principal of the human condition: plurality. Her judgement is not a legal judgement; it is levied against Eichmann and the court proceedings. For Arendt, justice is a matter of judgement, and she was concerned with the way post-war trials were being carried out as show trials, which claimed justice on one hand, while failing to try the crimes of the perpetrators on the other. Her point was that the judgement had already been rendered before the trial began. The trial itself served the purpose of providing a record and allowing individuals to testify. If trials are meant to try individuals and their actions through evidence and arguments that demonstrate the violation of the law, then the trial of Eichmann failed because Eichmann had not technically violated any laws; he was following laws that should have never been made.

That summer Gershom Scholem wrote to Hannah Arendt that her report of the trial left him with 'a feeling of rage and fury'. He was shocked by her tone and shocked by her willingness to mention Jewish complicity, specifically the role of the Jewish Councils in overseeing the selection process for deportation to concentration camps. Scholem could not understand Arendt's tone and the style she chose to write in:

> It is the heartless, the downright malicious tone you employ in dealing with the topic that so profoundly concerns the center of our life. There is something in the Jewish language that is completely undefinable, yet fully concrete – what the Jews call *ahavath Israel*, or love for the Jewish people. With you, my dear Hannah, as with so many intellectuals coming from the German left, there is no trace of it.[8]

Arendt responded:

> Let's get to the real issue. Tying in with what I just said, I'll begin
> with *ahavath Israel* . . . How right you are that I have no such
> love, and for two reasons: first, I have never in my life 'loved'
> some nation or collective – not the German, French, or American
> nation, or the working class, or whatever else there might be
> in this price range of loyalties. The fact is that I love only my
> friends and am quite incapable of any other sort of love.[9]

Arendt's response to Scholem is informed by two elements of
her political thinking: identity and love. Jewishness was a fact
of her existence, not the grounds for solidarity with a people or
movement. As she wrote in *The Human Condition*, love is apolitical,
because it turns one away from the world. Arendt echoes this
argument in a letter to the novelist James Baldwin written in
1962 about the solidarity of oppressed peoples: 'In politics, love
is a stranger, and when it intrudes upon it nothing is achieved
except hypocrisy.'[10] To have not spoken about the role of the
Jewish Councils would have been a betrayal of her obligation to
report the facts. But more importantly perhaps, in holding them
accountable she was treating them as full persons with a sense of
moral responsibility, unlike Eichmann, who was a banal buffoon
incapable of self-reflective thinking.

In writing *Eichmann in Jerusalem* Arendt was confronted with
several of the claims she had made in *The Origins of Totalitarianism*.
At the end of *Origins* she had described a new radical evil that
appeared with the emergence of totalitarianism, and this radical
evil was marked by the use of concentration camps that created
holes of oblivion: 'We may say that radical evil has emerged in
connection with a system in which all men have become equally
superfluous.' In witnessing the trial of Eichmann, Arendt saw that

holes of oblivion did not exist, because 'there are too many people in the world to make oblivion possible'. More importantly, Arendt came to the observation that radical evil does not exist. In seeing Eichmann, she saw that evil was, in fact, banal: 'I think that evil in every instance is only extreme, never radical: it has no depth, and therefore has nothing demonic about it. Evil can lay to waste the entire world, like a fungus growing rampant on the surface. Only the good is always deep and radical.'[11]

There are several common misconceptions about Arendt's *Eichmann in Jerusalem*, which she spent the next few years responding to in lectures, essays and articles. The first is what she meant by the banality of evil. Arendt addresses this question directly in a 1964 interview with Joachim Fest:

> Now, one misunderstanding is this: people thought that what is banal is also commonplace. But I thought . . . That wasn't what I meant. I didn't in the least mean that there's an Eichmann in all of us, that each of us has an Eichmann inside of him and the Devil knows what else. Far from it! I can perfectly well imagine talking to somebody, who says to me something that I've never heard before, so it's not in the least commonplace. And I say, 'That's really rubbish.' That's the sense in which I meant it.

Eichmann was not stupid, he knew what he was doing. Arendt's argument was that he lacked an expansive imagination, the ability to imagine the world from the perspective of another. She illustrates this point with a story she heard from the German author Ernst Jünger during the war about starving peasants:

> A peasant had taken in Russian prisoners of war straight from the camps, and naturally they were starving – you know how Russian prisoners of war were treated here. And he says to Jünger, 'Well, they're subhuman – and . . . like cattle! It's

easy to see: they eat the pigs' food' . . . 'It's sometimes as if the German people were being ridden by the Devil.' And he didn't mean anything 'demonic' by that. Look here, there's something outrageously stupid about this story. I mean the story itself is stupid. The man doesn't see that this is what starving people do. That anyone would behave like that. Still, there's something outrageous about this stupidity . . . Eichmann was rather intelligent, but in this respect he was stupid. It was his thickheadedness that was so outrageous, as if speaking to a brick wall. And that was what I actually meant by banality. There's nothing deep about it – nothing demonic! There's simply resistance ever to imagine what another person is experiencing, isn't that true?[12]

Eichmann was a clown to Hannah Arendt not because he was funny, but because he was irrational and lacked the capacity to think expansively. Arendt wanted to 'Destroy the legend of the greatness of evil, of the demonic force'. And in doing so she turned to a line from the poet Bertolt Brecht, who advises 'The great political criminals must be exposed and exposed especially to laughter,' the argument being that tragedy deals with suffering less seriously than comedy. For Arendt, the only way 'to keep your integrity under these circumstances' is to remember this and judge that, regardless of what great crimes Eichmann committed, he was still a clown. In this way laughter becomes a means to self-sovereignty, and a way to deny legitimacy to evil-doers.

Another common response to Arendt's argument about the banality of evil was that she was claiming anybody could have done what Eichmann did. For Arendt, this was a question of judgement, and in 1964 she delivered a radio talk addressing this accusation for the Third Programme of the BBC in London; a shortened transcript, titled 'Personal Responsibility under Dictatorship', was also published in *The Listener* (6 August 1964). Arendt draws a distinction between legal and moral issues, which are not the same, but they have a certain affinity for one another because they both presume the power of judgement. The distinction between legal and moral issues is important to the way Arendt thinks about the relationship between thinking and judging, because technically everything the Nazi regime did was legal – they were obeying the law. In this sense, Eichmann had not committed a crime in the way one might normally be accused of committing a crime, but obviously what he did was wrong. And the question of wrong is a question of moral not legal judgement. How do we hold someone personally accountable when they have violated a moral code and not a legal one?

In Arendt's judgement, Eichmann had not just violated the normative moral orders of society, because totalitarianism had exploded all pre-existing moral categories of judgement. Drawing a further distinction between personal responsibility and political responsibility, Arendt describes how there had been a near universal breakdown of personal judgement in Europe, and how, to a certain extent, everyone bears political responsibility. But she argues that a person cannot take responsibility for the sins of others. That is, one cannot feel guilty for something one has not done. And what happened in Germany was that those who did nothing wrong felt guilty, and those who did everything wrong, like Eichmann, felt no guilt at all.

For Arendt, the question was: What is the difference between those who participated and those who chose to resist? The answer is thinking. Those who did not participate were the ones who dared to think for themselves, and they were capable of doing so not because they had a better system of values or because the old standards of right and wrong were still applicable, but because they asked themselves to what extent they would still be able to live in peace with themselves after having committed certain deeds, and they decided that it would be better to do nothing, because that was the only way they could go on living. Those who did not 'go along' chose to think.

Eichmann in Jerusalem was not translated into Hebrew or available for purchase in Israel until 2000. Publishers in Israel refused to print it, and stores refused to sell it. Arendt was forced to personally ship copies to her friends. In a letter to Samuel Grafton, who was commissioned by the photo-magazine *Look* to cover the response to *Eichmann*, Arendt said she had three reasons for wanting to cover the trial:

> First, I wanted to see one of the chief culprits with my own eyes as he appeared in the flesh . . . Second, there exists a wide spread theory, to which I also contributed, that these crimes defy the possibility of human judgment and explode the framework of our legal institutions . . . and Third: I have been thinking for many years, or to be specific, for thirty years about the nature of evil, and the wish to expose myself not to the deeds which, after all, were well-known – but to the evil-doer himself, probably was the most powerful motive in my decision to go to Jerusalem.[13]

The reaction to Arendt's reportage was an important political phenomenon in itself. Grafton asked Arendt if she felt like the reaction to her book threw new light on the tensions in Jewish life and politics, and what she thought the real causes of the attacks were. Arendt said she felt like she had 'inadvertently touched upon the Jewish part of what the Germans call their "unmastered past"'. She added, 'It looks to me now as though this question was bound to come up anyhow and that my report crystallized it in the eyes of those who do not read big books (like Hilberg).' Arendt did not think there was a definitive answer to Grafton's first question, but she did think a coordinated attack had been mobilized by Jewish organizations who felt like they were under attack, because she touched on the role of Jewish leadership.

Eichmann in Jerusalem remains a controversial book more than fifty years after its initial publication. Arendt's arguments about the contours of human consciousness, morality and politics continue to provoke readers, but what really upsets people is Arendt's tone, for which she refused to apologize. In one interview she said, 'Well, there is nothing I can do about that.' The ironic tone of the work cannot be disentangled from the text. As with *Origins, The Human Condition* and *Between Past and Future,* Arendt did not separate form and content: she used form in relationship to content to illustrate her thinking and argument.

To Arendt the most upsetting part of the literary show trial was that she was pronounced guilty for a book she had never written. Most of her critics had, she wrote, not even bothered to read it. They objected to her ironic tone, not its content. Worst of all, they were more interested in invalidating her than engaging with her arguments.

Arendt's response was to neither submit to her sentence nor deny the onslaught of responses. Instead, she insisted on confronting the issue head-on. What most worried Arendt was a form of political propaganda that uses lies to erode reality. Political power, she warned, will always sacrifice factual truth for political gain. But the side effect of the lies and the propaganda that are necessary when rewriting history is the destruction of the common sense by which we take our bearings in the world.

The loss of truth in the public sphere poses a threat to political freedom. As Arendt realized, telling the truth about one's experiences in the public sphere is very dangerous. Truth-tellers have always stood outside the realm of politics, often as the subject of collective scorn. When asked towards the end of her life whether she would publish *Eichmann in Jerusalem* again despite all the trouble it brought her, she was defiant. She invoked, and then dismissed, the classic maxim 'Let justice be done, though the world perish.' Instead, she asked a question that seemed to her more urgent: 'Let truth be told though the world may perish?' Her answer was yes.

When Arendt left Jerusalem she went to Basel with Heinrich Blücher to meet Karl and Gertrud Jaspers. It was Heinrich's first trip to Europe since fleeing in 1941, and his first time meeting Jaspers in person. They had been corresponding since Arendt's first return trip to Europe some years earlier, when Jaspers was so taken by his impressions of Heinrich that he decided he had to write to him. When they left Basel they took a trip to Italy to visit Paestum and Syracuse. Arendt had fallen in love with the Greek and Roman ruins in Syracuse on her first trip to Palestine, and wanted to show them to Blücher.

When they returned home in autumn 1961 Blücher suffered an aneurysm. Arendt was teaching a course on Machiavelli at Wesleyan University in Connecticut while finishing *On Revolution*. Her close friend, the writer Charlotte Beradt, 'found him in a deranged state, covered with burns from his own cigarette, pacing back and forth over a chaos of papers, books, and overturned furniture'.[14] He was taken to Columbia Presbyterian Medical Center. Arendt called Mary McCarthy to take over her class and went to New York to care for her husband. When she arrived at the hospital, the neurologist gave her Blücher's prognosis, which she relayed to him: '50 per cent mortality in cases like this.' Heinrich responded, 'Reg Dich doch bloss nicht auf, Du vergisst die anderen 50 per cent' (Don't get upset, you forgot the other 50 per cent).

When Blücher was well enough to be on his own, Arendt returned to Connecticut for three days a week to teach, spending the rest of the time in New York with Blücher. By December she had finished *On Revolution* and was editing *Eichmann in Jerusalem*. In January 1962 she left for Chicago where she had lecture commitments, but health was not on their side. While lecturing she came down with a cold with respiratory complications, and had a bad allergic reaction to the antibiotics prescribed, leaving her barely able to finish her class. She returned to New York that March and was nearly killed when the taxi she was in was struck by a truck in Central Park. Arendt suffered a concussion, nine broken ribs, broken teeth, a near-broken wrist, multiple lacerations, haemorrhages of both eyes and heart-muscle damage related to shock.[15] Arendt recounted the accident to Mary McCarthy:

> When I awoke in the car [on the way to the hospital] and became conscious of what had happened, I tried out my limbs, saw that I was not paralyzed and could see with both eyes; then tried out my memory – very carefully, decade by decade, poetry, Greek and German and English; then telephone numbers. Everything is alright. The point was that for a fleeting moment I had the feeling that it was up to me whether I wanted to live or die. And though I did not think that death was terrible, I also thought that life was quite beautiful and that I rather like it. When I came to the hospital and the young, very competent neurosurgeon, who then operated on me, declared, 'It looks rather horrible but I think nothing serious has happened,' I was pretty sure that he was right. In the hospital, I came rather brutally face to face with our present day world from which we usually are shielded. Medically, things were quite good; but the administration and the nurses plus their aides plus the food incredibly outrageously bad. The whole place is run under the motto: We could not care less.[16]

Arendt was released after a couple of weeks in hospital.[17] Charlotte Beradt assured Mary McCarthy that Arendt was in good spirits the whole time, and was collecting flowers, telegrams, notes and letters 'like a child'. But their spate of bad luck followed them through the year. Blücher fell ill again the following autumn as Arendt was about to leave for Chicago, where she was scheduled to teach

'Introduction to Politics'. She ended up flying back to New York every other weekend to be with Heinrich and take care of him.

The fates eventually granted them a reprieve after the semester ended that spring. Blücher's health improved, and they were able to take a holiday together to Italy, Greece and Israel. Arendt describes their weeks together as living 'the easy life of the gods'. They spent their days viewing collections of antiquities, buying clothes, drinking Campari and wine, and eating. The only book Arendt read on their trip was Goethe's *Italienische Reise* (1817). She was, as she put it, on strike, and content to fill her days looking at the sights: 'Sicily – Syracuse in particular – was very beautiful. First the strange cathedral with the most wonderful Doric columns incorporated into it, Romanesque, and a late Baroque façade that is one of the most beautiful I have ever seen.' It was a moment of repose for Arendt and Blücher, an opportunity to slow down after nearly twenty years of concentrated writing, publishing, editing, teaching, travelling and illness.

16

On Revolution

In the autumn of 1963 Hannah Arendt and Heinrich Blücher
returned home, to the tumultuous landscape of American politics.
The United States was becoming further entrenched in the Vietnam
War, the Civil Rights movement was gaining momentum, and on
22 November President John F. Kennedy was assassinated in Dallas,
Texas. Arendt wrote to Karl Jaspers with a great sense of urgency:
'What is now in the balance is nothing more and nothing less than
the existence of the Republic.'[1]

Arendt was teaching at the University of Chicago when
Kennedy was assassinated. She watched the live television
coverage of his funeral with Mary McCarthy and Hans
Morgenthau. Arendt had voted for Kennedy in the election and
was hopeful that his campaign signalled the demise of political
party machinery. In an essay on the Kennedy–Nixon debates,
she writes: 'The 1960 nominations were foregone conclusions,
not because the conventions were rigged but because the vote-
getting capacities of the candidates had proved themselves in
the primaries and public opinion polls without the help of the
party machines.'[2] Arendt argued that the decline of political
parties would lead to independent voters having more power in
elections, and that the party machines made citizens impotent
by presenting them with the candidates who had the most power
within the machinery instead of allowing the people to decide on
their own.

Arendt's well-timed publication of *On Revolution* in 1963 was overshadowed by the clamour around *Eichmann in Jerusalem*. Arendt was inspired to write the book while at Princeton University in the spring of 1959, when she attended a conference on 'The United States and the Revolutionary Spirit'. The conference focused on the parallels 'between the American, French, and Russian revolution as opposing models of social change'. Princeton invited Fidel Castro, the prime minister of the newly formed Cuban government, to give the keynote address. According to another student in attendance, Castro talked about himself as a 'practical revolutionary', as 'someone who did not study but rather produced a revolution'. He thought that the Cuban Revolution was more in the tradition of the 1776 American Revolution than the 1789 French Revolution, or 1917 Russian Revolution, in part because it proved that 'it was possible to create a revolution when the people were not hungry'.[3] Arendt supported the Cuban Revolution, which had begun in the summer of 1953, and had written about it for the *Partisan Review* as an example of what happens 'when a poverty-stricken people' are 'released from the obscurity of their farms and homes' and 'permitted to show their misery' in public.

When Arendt lectured on revolution at the University of Chicago in 1966, she began with the reflection that her subject was 'embarrassingly topical'. Revolutions had become everyday occurrences in the twentieth century: the Cuban Revolution in 1953, the Hungarian Revolution in 1956, the Cuban Missile crisis in 1962, which Arendt called a 'quiet revolution', the military coups in Vietnam, South Korea and Greece, the Cultural Revolution in China, to name just a few. Revolutions, she claimed, are a sign of political decay, of the breakdown of authority and the loss of tradition, they mark a rupture and usher something new into the world.

On Revolution is a comparative study of the French and American revolutions. In Arendt's analysis, the French Revolution failed because it was motivated by the social question of poverty and by the sentiments of pity and empathy. As the French Revolutionaries found freedom in action in the public sphere, they were unable to establish a permanent space for speech and action, because solidarity with the people had been founded upon poverty, inequality and violence. Arendt did not think that social questions like poverty could be resolved by politics. For her, social questions are questions of economic distribution.

In her reading of the French Revolution, the attempt to solve social questions through political means only led to violence. Surveying the French, Cuban and Hungarian Revolutions, it appeared that 'liberation from necessity, because of its urgency, always takes precedence over the building of freedom.' As she had laid out in *The Human Condition*, freedom begins after the necessities of life have been met. Unlike France, America was not hindered by economic inequality, she argued. The fathers of the American Revolution were successful because they concerned themselves not with equality, but with the political question of freedom: 'The word "revolutionary" can be applied only to revolutions whose aim is freedom.'[4]

Revolutions establish political spaces for freedom where people can appear before one another as equal citizens. This conception of politics is rooted in Arendt's understanding of plurality. Plurality is a fact of human existence, the necessary condition for action, and is an experience of equality and distinction. This necessary condition of plurality for action is threatened by demands for social equality, which Arendt saw as a distinct feature of modernity. The rise of the social led to the breakdown of political institutions, by liberating private interests into the public sphere, levelling politics to economic interests.

In order to call something a revolution today, Arendt argued, it must found something new and it must be radical enough to change the whole fabric of government and/or society. Revolution is not simply a question of 'putting a different set of people at the head of the government or of permitting some segment of the population to rise into the public realm'. From these two conditions there are two forms of revolutions: social and political. Social revolutions change the fabric of society, which we see in the French Revolution and Marx's promise of a classless society; political revolutions found a new body politic, which we see with the American Revolution, which instituted a new form of government. For social and political revolutions, the breakdown of authority is the necessary condition, and no revolution can succeed where the loyalty of the armed forces, both police and army, remains intact. Such revolutions do not emerge from the disintegration of the body politic; in order for revolution to be successful there 'must also be men eager and prepared to take up themselves the responsibilities of power – waiting in the wings. These people in the 18th century were the *hommes de lettres* [men of letters].'5

Looking at the American Revolution, Arendt saw the possibility for a more democratic form of government that was rooted in local politics. She develops an idea of council systems out of her reading of Tocqueville in order to imagine a form of engaged citizenry that found happiness in public participation. A Constitutional Republic like the United States can guarantee the rights of citizens, but it is up to citizens to ensure those rights through political action. For Arendt, politics emerges not out of the courage of our convictions, which are easy, but out of the courage of our experiences that ground us in the everyday lives and habits of citizens. The experience of public happiness is essential to retaining the spirit of revolution.

She was critical of representational politics, because electing others to represent one's own self-interest allowed for a disavowal of democratic responsibility. And, as Arendt observed the transformation in American politics over the years, she saw how the political party machinery was increasingly making citizens impotent. The more people hand over their political power to parties, the less power they have in politics. And in this way, bureaucracy and interest groups overpower citizen engagement, and all joy in public life is lost.

One of the virtues of the American political system that Arendt praised was the separation of powers that came from the French philosopher Montesquieu, whom Arendt thought, along with Marx and Thomas Hobbes, was among the great thinkers of modernity. Montesquieu developed a conception of power that was not purely instrumental. In formulating the branches of government, he found a way to split power among 'the three main political activities of men: the making of laws, the executing of decisions, and the deciding judgment that must accompany both.'[6] Or, as we know it today: the legislative, the executive and the judiciary. Montesquieu's conception of political power resonated with Arendt's conception of plurality and political action.

But Arendt was not entirely hopeful about the future of American democracy. While she maintained that the American Revolution successfully founded a new body politic, she was worried about the continuing influence of the social question on the realm of politics. She saw American society succumbing to what she called the production of the 'waste economy' in which all activity is reduced to sheer instrumentalism for the sake of production and consumption. And, more importantly, the American Revolution might have established a new body politic, but it failed to preserve the spirit of revolution. The founders failed to protect the roots of power at the local level of government, and instead gave too much power to the state and federal levels of government. In other words, they removed the power from the people, limiting the potential for political action.

How can stable political institutions contain a revolutionary spirit? For Arendt, this was not a question to be solved, but rather an experience to understand. The stagnation of political

Hannah Arendt in Palenville, New York, 1966.

institutions can lead to instability, and in order for a vibrant polity to exist it must be invigorated by democratic participation.

Arendt spent the summer of 1966 at Chestnut Lawn House in Palenville, New York, a sprawling estate in the Catskills about forty minutes away from Bard College. For two months she relaxed reading Agatha Christie novels, Simenon's detective stories and Peter Nettl's two-volume biography of Rosa Luxemburg, which Robert Silvers at the *New York Review of Books* had suggested she review. She had also begun work on 'Truth and Politics' in response to the *Eichmann* scandal.

That autumn Arendt presented 'Truth and Politics' at Emory University, Eastern Michigan University, St John's College in Annapolis and Wesleyan University. The essay was eventually folded into an epilogue for a second edition of *Eichmann*, and a foreword for the German edition. She finished editing 'Truth and Politics' while teaching 'From Machiavelli to Marx' and 'Political Experiences in the Twentieth Century' at Cornell University that autumn, and delivered the final version as a keynote address at the 1966 American Political Science Association meeting.[7] Arendt received an overwhelmingly positive response to the essay. She told Jaspers: 'I am flooded with letters from all the Jewish organizations with invitations to speak, to appear at congresses, and so forth – even from those I have attacked. Also, the Hebrew edition of *Eichmann* is finally out in Israel. I think that the war between me and the Jews is over.'[8]

'Truth and Politics' begins with a footnote to the title. Arendt says that the essay was

caused by the so-called controversy after the publication of *Eichmann in Jerusalem*. Its aim is to clarify two different, though interconnected, issues of which I had not been aware before and whose importance seemed to transcend the occasion. The first concerns the question of whether it is always legitimate to tell the truth . . . the second arose through the amazing amount of lies used in the 'controversy' – lies about what I had written, on the one hand, and about the facts I had reported, on the other.[9]

Arendt was not defending herself against critique, she was trying to reckon with what happens when a person tries to negate another person's experiences of the world, which is what can happen when factual truth is introduced into the realm of politics. As she writes, truth and politics have never been on good terms with one another, and she felt bound to tell the truth *as she saw it*, which was not a foreclosure of other ways of seeing, but a way of recording her own experience in the world. 'No permanence, no perseverance in existence, can ever be conceived of without men willing to testify to what is and appears to them because it is.'[10]

The Eichmann controversy raised a number of questions that Arendt wanted to understand: What is the nature of truth? What happens to the political realm when truth is not regarded as a public virtue? And what happens to truth when it is rendered powerless in the public realm? Since Socrates, truth-tellers have stood outside the realm of politics. Seen this way, truth-telling is apolitical and dangerous, because it challenges those in power. In politics, there can only be opinion. In his Declaration of Independence of 1776, Jefferson said 'we hold these truths to be self-evident' because he was looking for consent, but in saying 'hold', in Arendt's reading, he conceded that the equality he spoke about was not self-evident at all, and that it was politically relevant only as a matter of opinion and not truth. But this presents an array of problems, one being the liar. When the liar cannot make his lie stick, he claims it is his mere opinion, and this argument is a form of action that alters the public realm. In a world where lies are being continuously subsisted for factual truth and truth is being defamed as lies, what is in question is our capacity to discern fact from fiction.

What is at stake in Arendt's essay is the existence of the world held in common. Arendt is concerned that factual truth is in great danger of disappearing from the world altogether, because it is more fragile than axioms or theories, which are produced by the human mind. Facts emerge from lived experience and events in the world, which means that they rely upon remembrance and storytelling in order to exist. If one begins rewriting the facts, they erase the world of shared human experience.

Throughout the essay Arendt emphasizes the relationship between plurality, the appearance of individuals in the public realm, and the necessity to engage in dialogue with opinions that are not our own. That is, we have to make public use of our private thoughts. Arendt ties the necessity of plurality in public life to the necessity of plurality in thinking, to illustrate how it is that we form different political opinions:

> The more people's standpoints I have present in my mind while I am pondering a given issue, and the better I can imagine how I would feel and think if I were in their place, the stronger will be my capacity for representative thinking and the more valid my conclusions, my opinion.[11]

Consistent lying pulls the ground out from under our feet and provides no other ground upon which to stand. Arendt ends her essay by answering the question 'What is truth?' 'Conceptually, we may call truth what we cannot change; metaphorically, it is the ground on which we stand and the sky that stretches above us.'[12] Truth gives us a sense of stability in the world, but like the ground and sky is always moving.

17

Men in Dark Times

Before Arendt travelled to Jerusalem in 1961 she had begun
preparing a course on the poet and playwright Bertolt Brecht.
The material from the course was eventually published in the *New
Yorker* in 1966, in *Men in Dark Times* with some revisions in 1968,
and in German for the journal *Merkur* in 1969.

When Arendt's essay on Brecht, 'What Is Permitted to Jove',
initially appeared in the *New Yorker* it was met with controversy.
Sidney Hook wrote, 'Only one word describes Hannah Arendt's
effort to obliterate Brecht's remark and to use it as an index for
his anti-Stalinist sentiments: *Unverschämtheit*, shamelessness.'
John Willett, a co-editor of Brecht's collected works in English,
responded by demanding Arendt hand over her sources
proving that Brecht had praised Stalin. Arendt did not respond
immediately, and when she did Willett was not satisfied with her
evidence. He penned an open letter to the *Times Literary Supplement*,
which was reported on by the *New York Times*. Arendt responded to
the interview request and assured readers she was 'quite satisfied'
with her work, and believed it to be accurate.

Arendt told her editor at the *New Yorker* that she had written
'the piece originally out of anger with a friend', Erich Heller, who
wanted 'to throw Brecht out the window' because of his sympathy
for Stalin. Heller had not understood Arendt's account of Brecht
either. He attacked her personally, arguing that her essay on Brecht
'may well be one of those occasions when Hannah Arendt put her

very great intelligence into the service of an erroneous judgment; and when this happened, she was never simply wrong, she exploded into wrongness, with angry sparks flying about'.[1]

Heller, Willett and Hook were responding to a footnote in Arendt's essay where she says,

> Brecht's praise of Stalin has been carefully eliminated from his *Collected Works*. The only traces are to be found in Prosa, vol. v, the posthumously published notes for Brecht's unfinished book *Me-ti*. There Stalin is praised as 'the useful one' and his crimes are justified. Immediately after his death, Brecht wrote that he had been 'the incarnation of hope' for 'the oppressed of five continents'.

Arendt did not condemn Brecht's sin. She did not believe that Brecht should be cast aside for his poor political decisions. He was a great poet, and that was the ground on which he was to be judged. Arendt accorded poets and poetry a distinct place in her understanding of the world, between the life of the mind and the life of action, and granted them reprieve from worldly obligation. 'Poets have not often made good, reliable citizens,' she wrote. Brecht was punished with a 'loss of talent' by the gods of poetry:

> Now reality overwhelmed him to the point where he could no longer be its voice; he had succeeded in being in the thick of it – and had proved that this is no good place for a poet to be. This is what the case of Bertolt Brecht is likely to teach us, and what we ought to take into consideration when we judge him today, as we must, and pay him our respect for all that we owe him. The poets' relation to reality is indeed what Goethe said it was: They cannot bear the same burden of responsibility as ordinary mortals; they need a measure of remoteness, and yet would not be worth their salt if they were not forever tempted

to exchange this remoteness for being just like everybody else. On this attempt Brecht staked his life and his art as few poets had ever done; it led him into triumph and disaster.

Arendt's argument was that poets deserve a 'certain latitude' in the public's consideration, because they are to a degree removed from the world of human affairs. Arendt admits that Brecht himself would refuse this kind of exception, but she also held that one must retain the ability to discern between political and moral judgements: 'Every judgment is open to forgiveness, every act of judging can change into an act of forgiving; to judge and to forgive are but the two sides of the same coin. But the two sides follow different rules.'[2] Arendt's judgement of Brecht is the judgement of a storyteller, not a moral arbiter. It is what some have called 'poetic judgement'. The cost of Brecht's failure was his gift, and this loss, for Arendt, illustrated 'how difficult it is to be a poet in this . . . or any other time'.[3]

After the publication of three books in four years, Arendt turned her attention to teaching, lecturing and writing essays. She joined Columbia University's Seminars, was a member of the *American Scholar* editorial board, attended forums at the Institute for Policy Studies in Washington, DC, represented the University of Chicago's Committee on Social Thought to the Presidential Office of Science and Technology, joined the Board of the National Translation Center, and was a consultant for the National Endowment for the Humanities, the National Book Award Committee and PEN International. She was also the chairperson for the Spanish Refugee Aid organization, which involved raising money to build a Spanish refugee centre in Montauban and writing memos about the Spanish refugees in France and Algiers.[4]

In 1968, as she was beginning to think about *The Life of the Mind*, Arendt published two collected volumes of work: *Illuminations*, which was the first English-language publication of Walter Benjamin's work, and *Men in Dark Times*, a collection of essays on twentieth-century thinkers. Both works were offerings of friendship. Arendt's introductory essay for *Illuminations*, 'Walter Benjamin', was published in both volumes. She had been concerned about the publication of Benjamin's work at the hands of Theodor Adorno and Max Horkheimer at the Institute for Social Research, and wanted to bring his work to a public audience. Arendt could not write her essay about Benjamin in English. She wrote it in German and had it translated by Harry Zohn, who was translating Benjamin's work for the volume. Arendt's affection for Benjamin resounds throughout her essay, and it is clear that she felt a personal responsibility to shepherd his work, which he had entrusted to her and others for safekeeping.[5]

Arendt published *Men in Dark Times* the following autumn. The title was inspired by Bertolt Brecht's poem 'To Those Born Later', which begins: 'Truly, I live in dark times!' Brecht wrote the poem in exile shortly before the outbreak of war. On the surface the subjects of Arendt's collection have little in common with one another: Hermann Broch, Bertolt Brecht, Walter Benjamin, Randall Jarrell, Rosa Luxemburg, Isak Dinesen, Lessing (the only one not from the twentieth century) and Pope John XXIII. But as one reads through the collection they are returned to the core elements of Arendt's thinking: plurality, conversation, poetry, durability, thinking, judgement, storytelling and love. At the same time, the text offers an intimate portrait of what it means to be human in dark times. In this darkness she found a form of illumination known by those pariahs who have been forced to wander the earth looking for a home in a world. 'Even in the darkest of times,' Arendt writes, 'we have the right to expect some illumination.' This illumination is a kind of beauty found in the life and work of some men and women who have given voice to their experiences. But this humanity, Arendt writes, is dearly bought:

it is often accompanied by so radical a loss of the world, so fearful an atrophy of all the organs with which we respond to it – starting with the common sense with which we orient ourselves in a world common to ourselves and others and going on to the sense of beauty, or taste, with which we love the world.

Men in Dark Times offers a series of meditative portraits on the kinds of goodness and warmth generated among persecuted peoples. The collection of essays, written for various occasions, includes book reviews, introductory texts and profiles published mostly in the *New Yorker* and the *New York Review of Books*. In her introduction to the volume, Arendt frames the book by saying, 'this collection of essays and articles is primarily concerned with persons – how they lived their lives, how they moved in the world, and how they were affected by historical time.'[6] After reading the collection, Mary McCarthy said she was struck by the 'folkishness' of the portraits. She thought there was a gnomic quality in them, something of a woodcut.[7] McCarthy read the essays as runic tales offering character lessons for how to live. And much to the point, she argued that what connected Arendt's woodcuts was the role friendship played in each of their lives, and how each became a travelling companion for the other. Arendt agreed with McCarthy that there was a 'fairy-tale quality' about her portraits. Arendt had imagined the portraits as 'silhouettes' in which each person treasures the importance of friendship.[8]

For Arendt, conversation was the lifeblood of friendship. 'Gladness, not sadness,' she writes, 'is talkative, and truly human dialogue differs from mere talk or even discussion in that it is entirely permeated by pleasure in the other person and what he says.' Aside from Arendt's husband Heinrich Blücher, no one understood this better than her mentor Karl Jaspers. Notably, *Men in Dark Times* includes two essays on Jaspers. The first is a 'Laudatio' delivered when Jaspers was awarded the German Book Trade's Peace Prize, and the second is a reflective essay on Jaspers's work titled 'Karl Jaspers: Citizen of the World?' In Jaspers Arendt found a man who understood the art of listening and conversation, and elevated these worldly activities to the centre of his life and work:

> Within this small world he unfolded and practiced his incomparable faculty for dialogue, the splendid precision of his way of listening, the constant readiness to give a candid account of himself, the patience to linger over a matter under discussion, and above all the ability to lure what is otherwise passed over in silence into the area of discourse, to make it worth talking about. Thus in speaking and listening, he succeeds in changing, widening, sharpening – or, as he himself would beautifully put it, in illuminating.

For Arendt, Karl Jaspers embodied what it meant to think, because they both understood the importance of conversation, lingering over topics and returning to subjects of contemplation.

Arendt saw Jaspers in Basel for the last time in autumn 1968 after the publication of *Men in Dark Times*. He and his wife Gertrud were in good spirits and 'intellectually lively'. They had coffee and talked for hours on end, and she found it easy to converse with him, despite the gaps in his memory. She writes to Blücher,

> Jaspers, same as always, [is] easier to bear than a year ago because he is no longer trying to hide or conceal anything. He is now fully aware of his decline, even though at times he absolutely won't accept it. Everything is much easier because it isn't necessary to pretend anymore. That's how it is. But he still enjoys life. He says: Life was beautiful. I say: I know you still think: Life is beautiful. He says: You're right.[9]

When Arendt returned to New York to teach a course on 'Politics and Philosophy' at the New School for Social Research, she wrote a letter to Jaspers for his 86th birthday. She lamented not being able to join the celebrations and wished she could have seen him. Three days later, on 26 February 1969, Karl Jaspers died. Gertrud sent a short telegram to friends: 'Today my life's companion Karl Jaspers died.' It was Gertrud's birthday.

Jaspers's death did not come as a surprise to Arendt. She knew that he had been sick for some time, and had been relieved that he had accepted his illness. But none of this took away from the loss, which she had dreaded, thinking that each visit to see him might be her last. Arendt flew to Basel for the funeral service on 4 March and spoke about 'Jaspers's life and writing, of Jaspers as a philosopher and a citizen':

> We do not know, when a man dies, what has come to pass. We know only: he has left us. We depend upon his works, but we know that the works do not need us. They are what the one who dies leaves in the world – the world that was there before he came and which remains when he has gone. What will become of them depends on the way of the world. But the simple fact that these books were once a lived life, this fact does not go directly into the world or remain safe from forgetfulness. That about a man which is most impermanent and also perhaps most great, his spoken word and his unique comportment, that dies with him and thus needs us; needs us who think of him. Such thinking brings us to a relationship with the dead one, out of which, then, conversation about him springs and sounds again in the world. A relationship with the dead one – this must be learned, and, in order to begin this, we come together now, in our shared sorrow.[10]

Arendt observed Jaspers's passing with her own personal *Shiva*, wearing black for an extended period of mourning, with brightly coloured scarves. Jaspers's disappearance from the world meant the physical disappearance of her mentor and friend.

After Jaspers's funeral Arendt returned home to Heinrich, who was forced to retire from Bard College in 1968 because of his own declining health. She also returned home to the storm of the student protest movements, which they watched on television from their living room on the Upper West Side.

18

Crises of the Republic

During a panel discussion at the 21st Street Theater of Ideas in 1969, Hannah Arendt discussed the loss of American faith in political institutions: 'It is obvious that the people in America no longer support the government . . . and it turns out that this form of government cannot truly govern without the support of the people.'[1] The American system of government rests upon the division of powers, and Arendt saw how this was being eroded through the rise of political parties, gradual centralization of government and the expansion of executive authority.

The ideas explored here became the basis for *Crises of the Republic*, a collection of essays that examine the contemporary ailments of democracy in America in historical and theoretical detail, focusing on Nixon and the Pentagon Papers in 'Lying in Politics', the protest movements in 'Civil Disobedience', the use of violence as a political instrument in 'On Violence', and an interview with the German journalist Adelbert Reif titled 'Thoughts on Politics and Revolution'.

'On Violence' was originally published as a special supplement titled 'Reflections on Violence' in the 27 February 1969 issue of the *New York Review of Books*. It was so popular when it appeared that the United States Army was unable to find a copy. Arendt published it as a standalone volume in 1970, and included it in *Crises of the Republic*, which appeared in 1972. In the essay Arendt dissects the three common theoretical justifications for the use of political violence: Marx's claim that violence is a necessary part of a society's revolutionary birth pains; Georges Sorel's claim that violence is essentially creative and therefore the proper mode for society's producers, the working class, as opposed to society's consumers; and Sartre's claim that violence is essential to man's creation and is 'man recreating himself'.[2]

Arendt was opposed to violent political action because violence destroys power, and the aim of politics and political protest is the creation of power. Arendt's understanding of power is bound up with her understanding of action, which she developed in her earlier writing on *The Human Condition* and *On Revolution*. Power corresponds with the human ability to act in concert with others and is world building, whereas violence is instrumental. It is a tool used to achieve forcibly a certain end. 'Violence', Arendt writes, 'can only destroy power. Out of the barrel of a gun grows the most effective command, resulting in the most instant and perfect obedience.' When violence is used by political leaders, it does not enhance their power, but diminishes it.

On 17 December 1967 she participated in a panel discussion on 'The Legitimacy of Violence', chaired by Robert Silvers of the *New York Review of Books*, with Noam Chomsky, Conor Cruise O'Brien and Robert Lowell at the 21st Street Theater for Ideas. From the audience Susan Sontag intervened in the discussion: 'It's personally hard for me to understand how in December 1967 in New York the discussion has at no point turned actively to the question of whether we, in this room, and people we know are going to be engaged in violence.'[3] Weighing power, force and violence, Arendt maintained that violence always rises out of impotence, and that it was important to draw a distinction between power and violence if one wanted to engage in effective political action. If the aim of politics is to generate power, and violence destroys power, then violence cannot be an efficacious political tool.

Arendt agreed with Chomsky that non-violence was essential to the Civil Rights movement for tactical reasons. She saw non-violence as a legitimate political tactic that could be utilized as a subversive instrument to hold the government accountable, but she wholly rejected the idea that protests should be used to challenge the foundations of the Republic.

Tom Hayden, a founder of Students for a Democratic Society, opposed Arendt's position, arguing that her remarks did not bear upon the present political conditions of injustice in America and were theoretical in nature: 'It seems to me that until you can begin to show – not in language, not in theory, but in action – that you can put an end to the war in Vietnam, and an end to American racism, you can't condemn the violence of those who can't wait for you.' Hayden thought there was a place for violence within the student protest movements, and that sometimes violence was a necessary response when the tactics of non-violence failed.

Arendt was supportive of the student protests at Columbia University when they began in 1968. She criticized the corporate influence on universities, the effect trustees had on faculty governance and the burgeoning of bureaucratic structures that undermined institutional integrity. Arendt supported students' demands that Columbia divest from the Institute for Defense Analysis, which conducted war-related research, and she attended the first day of protests on 4 April with Chanan Klenbort as the students occupied the buildings. 'The students are demonstrating and we are all with them,' she said.

Arendt saw the students taking personal, moral responsibility for unjust political conditions when university institutions failed to do so, but she quickly became disenchanted with the protests. The students had turned their gaze away from the actions of the institution to the institution itself. Arendt had initially supported the slogan Black Power, because she saw people coming together to act in concert and generate power: 'I thought the growth of black power could help lead to normal integration of blacks into the American group-power-interplay process.' But by the time she wrote 'On Violence', she was critical of the student protest movements and the use of violence as a political tactic by groups like the Black Panthers. She contended that black students had been 'admitted without academic qualification, and regarded and organized themselves as an interest group, the representatives of the black community'. She thought that it was a disservice to cave in to student demands for open admissions and Black Studies programmes. For her these were what she called 'nonexistent subjects', and she thought they would become a 'trap' used by white people to prevent black people from 'acquiring an adequate education'. These conclusions echo the argument she made in 'Reflections on Little Rock' and her letter to James Baldwin. They also echo her position towards feminism and Zionism. Politics organized around identity cannot sustain or confer political freedom, because it tries to create a universal subject. Any form of identity politics was a contradiction in terms for Arendt, who drew a sharp distinction between *who* a person is and *what* a person is. Nobody belongs to a political movement, Arendt argued, just because they are born black, Jewish or female.

In the autumn of 1970, as the protest movements died down, Arendt began preparing *The Life of the Mind*, while teaching a seminar on Immanuel Kant's *Critique of Judgement* at the New School for Social Research. On 30 October 1970 she delivered a keynote address on 'Thinking and Moral Considerations' at the annual meeting of the Society for Phenomenology and Existential Philosophy. It was a festive evening, and after the lecture her friend the philosopher Glenn Gray returned home with Arendt and Blücher for dinner and a nightcap. They ate, drank and spoke about the evening, but Blücher was not feeling well. He had started having chest pains earlier in the day, but did not think much of them. By the next afternoon, as Arendt and Blücher ate lunch, the pains returned and he was barely able to make it to the couch before he suffered a massive heart attack. Arendt called for an ambulance and held his hand as they waited for help to arrive. Blücher was very calm, and he told her quietly, 'This is it.' When he arrived at the hospital, he was in acute distress. The chest pains did not abate, and for six and a half hours the doctors worked on his heart.

Heinrich Blücher died on the evening of 31 October at Mount Sinai Hospital. He was 71 years old. Lotte Köhler, who had accompanied Arendt and Blücher through so many years of their marriage, took Arendt home and sent a simple telegram to their friends: 'Heinrich died Saturday of a heart attack. Hannah.'

The poet Randall Jarrell said their marriage had been a 'dual monarchy'. There was a genuine sense of excitement between them, and together they nurtured one another's passion for the life of the mind. Blücher did not leave behind a body of written work. Like Jaspers his great talent was for conversation, debate, friendship and teaching. They never had children because, as Arendt once told Hans Jonas, 'when we were young enough to have children, we had no money, and when we had money, we were too old.' Blücher explained their situation to his mother a bit differently: 'We decided not to have children in times such as these. We are sad about it, but a sense of responsibility for those who might be innocent sufferers is a valuable thing.'

Blücher had feared that his mother's mental illness might be congenital, and that the inherited aneurism he had suffered from as a young man might mark a child of his for a short or sickly life. Arendt knew herself well enough to realize that her passion for work and her need for quiet would make child-rearing onerous. But it was 'times such as these' that most strongly argued against children; many of their nearest friends, their tribe members, either remained childless or had their children only after emigration had brought them a measure of safety.[4]

Anne Weil in Hannah Arendt's apartment at 370 Riverside Drive, New York, *c.* 1971.

Blücher's funeral was held at the Riverside Chapel on 4 November 1970. Arendt had initially wanted a Jewish service for him, and to recite the Mourner's Kaddish, but instead a simple service with remembrances was settled upon. Blücher's colleagues at Bard College, Horace Kallen, the poet Ted Weiss and Irma Brandeis spoke, and after the service their tribe congregated at 370 Riverside Drive. Mary McCarthy and Anne Weil flew in from Paris to stay with Arendt for the better part of the winter.

Arendt was quiet in her mourning. She tells Mary McCarthy:

The truth is that I am completely exhausted, if you understand
by that no superlative of tiredness. I am not tired, or much
tired, just exhausted. I function alright now but know that
the slightest mishap can throw me off balance. I do not think
I told you that for ten years I had been constantly afraid that
just such a sudden death would happen. This fear frequently
bordered on real panic. Where the fear was, and the panic,
is now sheer emptiness. Sometimes I think without this
heaviness inside me I can no longer walk. And it is true I feel
like I am floating. If I think even a couple of months ahead
I get dizzy. I am now sitting in Heinrich's room and using

Hannah Arendt and Mary McCarthy in Sicily, 1971.

his typewriter. Gives me something to hold on to. The weird thing is that at no moment am I actually out of control.[5]

Arendt's first entry in her thinking journal after Blücher's death reads: 'Free, like a leaf in the wind.' After his death there is no record of Arendt's thinking journals. The last two are simply lists of dates and travels. When Blücher's stone was set in the faculty cemetery at Bard College, Arendt had a modest concrete bench installed where she could visit him each year on the anniversary of his death. Even after he was gone, their conversation continued.

The spring after Blücher's death Arendt travelled to Sicily with Mary McCarthy and her husband James West. The trip was so pleasant that when they returned Arendt decided to spend a month with McCarthy and West at their house in Castine, Maine. McCarthy made her a bedroom in the apartment above their garage and supplied it with Arendt's favourite breakfast foods: eggs, ham, cold cuts, bread, anchovy paste, coffee, grapefruit, orange juice. But Arendt was not ready for such closeness and seemed put off by how McCarthy knew her so well. During this time McCarthy described Arendt as being surrounded by friends, but riding 'like a solitary passenger on her train of thought'.

In *The Life of the Mind*, which Arendt had begun working on in 1968, she discusses the two-in-one conversation, that is the inner dialogue one has with one's self. In thinking, Arendt argued, one is never really alone. In the words of Cicero: 'Never am I more active than when I am doing nothing, never am I less alone than when I am by myself.' For Arendt, *The Life of the Mind* was a return to the tradition of philosophy which she had left in 1933. It was a chance to come face-to-face not with the evil doer himself, but with the question of why people are capable of doing evil at all. The three-part work was to be her crowning achievement.

19

The Life of the Mind

The final years of Hannah Arendt's life were dedicated to *The Life of the Mind*. In January 1970, a couple of months after Blücher's death, Arendt gave a lecture on 'Thought and Moral Propositions' at Loyola University, before going to deliver three public lectures at the University of Chicago titled 'Thought on Moral Propositions'. These lectures became 'Thinking and Moral Considerations', which was initially published in *Social Research* in the autumn of 1971. Arendt dedicated the essay to W. H. Auden in honour of his 65th birthday.

In 'Thinking and Moral Considerations' Arendt addresses the relationship between one's ability to think and make judgements. The question at the centre of the essay is: Can thinking condition us against evil doing? If it can, Arendt reasoned, then everyone must be capable of thinking; it cannot be relegated to the privileged few.

Arendt understands thinking to be a worldly activity that is about making meaning, unlike the urge to know or the acquisition of truth. In order to illustrate the activity of thinking, Arendt turns to Socrates, the thinker par excellence, and the similes he uses to describe himself: the stingray who paralyses, forcing one to stop, the gadfly who arouses one to thought, and the wind egg that is an empty idea, which means one must begin again. For Socrates, and Arendt, the work of understanding and creation of meaning is bound to eros, a kind of love that desires what it does not have:

Love, by desiring what is not there, establishes a relationship with it. To bring this relationship into the open, make it appear, men speak about it in the same way the lover wants to speak about his beloved. Since the quest is a kind of love and desire, the objects of thought can only be lovable things – beauty, wisdom, justice, etc.[1]

Arendt follows Socrates' argument to say we cannot become evil through thinking, because we can only think about virtues, and we become what we think about. It follows then that evil is not something that can be thought, because evil is not a virtue. The danger of non-thinking in political and moral affairs is that it teaches people to hold fast to whatever the prescribed rules of conduct may be at a given time in society. People get used to the rules, and so they get used to never making up their own minds. The faster someone holds to an old code or social norm, the more eager they will be to assimilate to a new one, which they won't even be aware of, because they're asleep.[2] In McCarthy's edits on the *New Yorker* print editions of 'Thinking' she crosses out unthinking and

Hannah Arendt teaching at the New School for Social Research, late 1960s.

writes 'evil'. In order to understand why evil exists in the world, and why some people go along with forces of evil, Arendt turned her attention to the activity of thinking, and the faculty of imagination.

Arendt had begun working on *The Life of the Mind* in 1968, and intended to write three volumes: *Thinking, Judging* and *Willing*. She tells McCarthy:

> I am not preparing a bomb by any means. Unless you would call preparations for writing about Thinking-Judging-Willing (a kind of part II to *The Human Condition*) preparing a bomb. On the contrary. I have a feeling of futility in everything I do. Compared to what is at stake everything looks frivolous. I know this feeling disappears once I let myself fall into that gap between past and future which is the proper temporal locus of thought.[3]

In the *Life of the Mind*, Arendt rejects the traditional dichotomy between the *vita activa* and the *vita contemplativa* in order to show how thinking is an activity in itself. Unlike the urge to know, or speculation of truth, thinking has to do with how one makes meaning from their experiences in the world.

Arendt tells McCarthy *The Life of the Mind* will be her 'crowning achievement'. She was finally joining the ranks of those who had for some time been engaged in the 'dismantling of metaphysics, and philosophy with all its categories'. Like Heidegger, Arendt wanted to escape the knot borne from the Western tradition, but, unlike Heidegger, for her it was possible only because the tradition had been broken, and there was no hope for renewing it. She was not seeking a new language with which to understand the meaning of being, she was looking for the question of meaning itself, and the nature of thinking.

In the autumn of 1971, while Arendt continued to work on the 'Thinking' portion of *The Life of the Mind*, she taught a course on

'The History of the Will' at the New School for Social Research and began drafting 'Willing'. In addition to her writing schedule, it was a busy time filled with dinners, meetings, honorary awards and lectures, including a party at the home of Dorothy Norman for Indira Gandhi, the prime minister of India.[4] Arendt's hectic schedule often left her tired, but she refused to cut back, even after her doctor diagnosed her with angina and advised she do less. Arendt told Mary McCarthy that she refused to live for her health. Giving up smoking and parties was not in her best interest. A small reprieve came when the German Supreme Court granted Arendt's application for restitution that she had filed years earlier. The court established her academic career had been definitively interrupted by the rise of Nazi Germany in 1933. Arendt used her restitution money to hire a personal secretary to type her correspondence, and a personal waiter and maid to help out with the entertaining. She also reserved a room for the summer of 1972 at the Casa Barbatè in Tegna, Switzerland, to work on *The Life of the Mind*.[5]

While Arendt was in Switzerland that July, she received a contract from Harcourt Brace Jovanovich for *The Life of the Mind*, and was invited to deliver the prestigious Gifford Lectures on Natural Theology at the University of Aberdeen, Scotland, the following spring, from April to May 1973. Arendt used the invitation to work on 'Thinking', preparing a total of ten lectures divided into four parts. She delivered the first lectures in April and May of 1973, and began with the clarification that she had neither a claim nor an ambition to be a philosopher, or what Kant called a 'professional thinker'. She had no intention of becoming a moral philosopher who would offer a theorem for how to be in the world. So she approached her task ironically, stating: 'The question is not whether political philosophy can make a contribution to political life, but whether philosophy can make a contribution to politics.'

Hannah Arendt in Tegna, Switzerland, 1969.

Arendt tells the audience that there are two rather different origins for her work on 'Thinking'. The first came from attending the trial of Adolf Eichmann in Jerusalem, and her work on the banality of evil. Arendt wanted to answer the question: Can the activity of thinking condition people in a way so that they abstained from evil-doing? And the second origin emerged from *The Human Condition*, which dealt with the life of action. The problem, as Arendt saw it, was that the activities of human life had only been addressed from the perspective of the *vita contemplativa*, which saw contemplation not as an activity but as a passivity, where mental activity comes to rest. Arendt wanted to look at the activity of thinking from a new point of view, in order to show how thinking was not a passivity but an inner experience.

Arendt was never wanting for admirers, but in the years after Blücher's death she grew closer to two men in particular, the poet W. H. Auden, whom she had known for some time, and Hans Morgenthau, one of her dear friends and colleagues from the University of Chicago. Three weeks after Blücher's death, Auden unexpectedly proposed marriage one evening when he arrived for an after-dinner drink. His proposal was platonic – a suggestion that they take care of one another in old age. Arendt told McCarthy,

> He came looking so much like a clochard that the doorman accompanied him. He said he had come back to New York only because of me, and that I was of great importance to him, that he loved me very much . . . I had to turn him down . . . I am almost beside myself when I think of the whole matter . . . I hate, am afraid of, pity, always have been, and I think I never knew anybody who aroused my pity to this extent.[6]

Arendt was surprised by Auden's proposal, not because of its platonic nature, but because she did not count him as an intimate among her 'tribe'. As she would write after his death,

> I met Auden late in his life and mine – at an age when the easy, knowledgeable intimacy of friendships formed in one's youth can no longer be attained, because not enough life is left, or expected to be left, to share with another. Thus, we were very good friends but not intimate friends.[7]

Her rebuff did not hinder their friendship, which possessed a kind of poetic durability. She might not have thought of him as a part of her 'tribe', but his companionship was an enduring part of her life.

When she finished the first series of lectures in Aberdeen, she returned to Tegna to work on 'Willing' before taking a two-week holiday with Hans Morgenthau on the Greek island of Rhodes. Arendt and Morgenthau had met in the early 1950s at the University of Chicago and developed a close friendship. Morgenthau was 'struck' the first time he met Arendt: 'the vitality of her mind, quick – sometimes too quick – sparkling, seeking, and finding the hidden meanings and connections beneath the surface of man and things.'

He mused that 'as others enjoy playing cards or the horses for their own sake, so Hannah Arendt enjoyed thinking.'

Throughout the many years of their friendship they provided intellectual companionship for one another. He had sat with her at the University of Chicago faculty club when she was shunned by her colleagues after the publication of *Eichmann*, and he defended her in the *New York Times* when she was attacked. Arendt remained by his side through a series of illnesses, and defended him when his reputation was under siege because of his opposition to the Vietnam War. They celebrated New Year's Eve watching Kennedy's funeral together, and travelled together in Greece. A close of friend of Morgenthau's wrote of them: 'My hunch is that each of them thought it would solve many problems if they were able to love

W. H. Auden in Hannah Arendt's apartment at 370 Riverside Drive, New York, 1967.

the other, but neither one did or could, yet each believed himself (herself) to be loved and desired by the other.'[8]

It is not clear from correspondence what was shared between them in private, but there is a period of time where Arendt signs her notes to Morgenthau with 'love', a salutation rarely seen in her letters. The limits of whatever this love was revealed themselves, however, on their trip to Rhodes, when Morgenthau proposed marriage. Arendt said no. Morgenthau pleaded with Arendt in a handwritten note:

Dear Hannah: Please don't mention your age to me again. It detracts from you, from me, and from our relationship. I love you at your age. I would love you at any age. I would love you if you were twenty. I would love you if you were ninety. Each time in a way appropriate to your age. This is a sacred thing, which we ought not to belittle or, rather, do it an injustice by confusing it with our age. Hans.[9]

But Arendt could not be swayed. She returned to Tegna to continue working on *The Life of the Mind*.

Arendt returned to New York that autumn amidst the Watergate scandal and President Nixon's resignation. As she wrote and spoke about 'Lying in Politics' and Watergate, she continued preparing 'Willing' while teaching courses on Greek political theory at the New School for Social Research. She was also preparing to sell her home at 370 Riverside Drive and thinking about retiring. But then something unexpected happened. Arendt had anticipated Jaspers's death, and even Blücher's, but she was not prepared for the sudden loss of Auden, her dishevelled friend and conversational companion. Shaken by the loss, Arendt openly wept while teaching one of her classes before Auden's memorial service at the Cathedral of St John the Divine.

Auden's service honoured his life as a poet. The choir sang the Anglican chant of Psalm 130, and performed Benjamin Britten's 'Offertory Anthem'. Robert Penn Warren read Auden's 'Missing', Galway Kinnel 'September 1, 1939', and William Meredith read 'In Memory of W. B. Yeats'. Auden's friends came together to recount his life's work, and in her own mourning for Auden, Arendt reread his poetry in chronological order, and was struck by the misery that had accompanied him throughout his life:

> Time and again when to all appearances he could not cope any more, when his slum apartment was so cold that the water no longer functioned and he had to use the toilet in the liquor store at the corner, when his suit – no one could convince him that a man needed at least two suits so that one could go to the cleaner or two pairs of shoes so that one pair could be repaired, a subject of an endlessly ongoing debate between us throughout the years – was covered with spots or worn so thin that his trousers would suddenly split from top to bottom, in brief, whenever disaster hit before your very eyes, he would begin to kind of intone an utterly idiosyncratic, absurdly eccentric version of 'count your blessings'.

Auden did not think happiness could be measured by worldly goods; he was not interested in the accumulation of things. 'Nobody I know wants to be buried / with a silver cocktail-shaker' he writes in one poem. Arendt found a kindred spirit in Auden who was always able to see the beauty in life through his love of language. She connected the dire conditions of Auden's material existence to his knowing ways 'in the infinite varieties of unrequited love'. He knew how to make a mess of things, and his surroundings mirrored a tendency towards self-destruction. In Arendt's approximation, what made Auden a poet was his love of words. And it was precisely this 'vulnerability to the crookedness of the desires, to the infidelities of the heart, to the injustices of the world' that made him a great poet. Through his verse Auden never parted ways with common sense or reason, instead he brought sanity to the madness of the world with his charming and often devastating lines.

That winter Arendt submitted the outline for the second series of Gifford Lectures on 'Willing', working out the different sections of the manuscript, amidst her usual teaching schedule. 'Willing' was the most difficult part of the manuscript for Arendt to write. Unlike thinking, the will is self-determined and autonomous, because it makes use of de-sensed thought objects, prepared by the thinking faculty. And in this way, the will is independent of both thinking and judging. Whereas 'Thinking' is characterized by the necessity of harmony for the two-in-one, 'Willing' is characterized as inharmonious. The activity of willing requires contest, and splits the self into two or more parts, pulling it in different directions. The will generates power to affect the future, yet it is only with the cessation of willing that the individual self is able to repair into one, appear in the world and act.

By the time she arrived in Aberdeen in May 1974 to lecture on 'Willing', she was tired. After Blücher's death Arendt had said that she wasn't tired, but exhausted from mourning. Now, after so many losses in such a short time, with the endless chaos of American politics, and her teaching and lecturing schedule, she was tired too. As Arendt got up to the podium to deliver the first lecture she suffered a nearly fatal heart attack. A friend in the audience rushed to her aid, and she was taken to the nearest hospital. Lotte Köhler flew in from New York and Mary McCarthy came from Paris. Her tribe found her in Scotland and spirited her to recovery. But again, Arendt refused to quit smoking, she refused to eat sensibly, she refused to drink less coffee. Arendt refused to live life in order to preserve mere existence. The one adjustment she consented to making was cutting back her teaching and lecturing schedule. She arranged for an early retirement from the New School for Social Research for the following year, and agreed to give one last year-long seminar on *The Life of the Mind*.

When she was released from the hospital on 27 May she went to London with Mary McCarthy before travelling to Tegna with their friend Elke Gilbert, who ensured that she arrived safely. Tegna was a refuge for Arendt, and she took her usual room at the Casa Barbatè. When she was settled, and feeling in good health, she received visitors: Robert Gilbert, Anne Weil, Hans Jonas and Hans Morgenthau. She filled her days with work and saw friends in the evening. After a month of rest Arendt decided to visit Heidegger in Freiburg against her doctor's orders. It was a frustrating visit for Arendt. Despite her ill health, Elfriede would not leave them alone. She had hoped to talk with Heidegger about *The Life of the Mind*, but she was barely allowed a moment to speak with him.

The Aberdeen lectures were postponed to the following year and Arendt returned home to New York at the end of the summer, frustrated by her time in Europe. She taught and worked on her book during the day, and received friends and students for dinner in the evenings.

In the spring of 1975 Arendt received the Sonning Prize from the Danish government for Contributions to European Civilization, and was invited to give the Atherton Lecture on Socrates at Harvard University. When she finished she travelled to the German Literature Archive in Marbach, to spend four weeks in June organizing Karl Jaspers's papers. When Arendt first arrived she was in great spirits. Friends recall her standing up in the cafeteria during lunch and reciting Friedrich Schiller by heart. But as the month wore on she became increasingly tired. She was not used to spending entire days indoors in libraries, and when Mary McCarthy came to visit she found her irritable and worn out.

Arendt left the archive and made her way to Tegna, taking her usual room at the Casa Barbatè. Her desk faced a 'deep valley and snow-covered alpine peaks'. She worked on her critique of Heidegger for 'Willing' and travelled to visit him in Freiburg again, despite the frustrations of her previous visit. This time she was able to talk to him, but found him 'suddenly really very old' and 'very deaf and remote'. She writes to McCarthy that she feels 'surrounded by old people who suddenly got very old'. She tells her that during her trip her first husband, Günther Anders, reappeared as well, also in 'very bad shape', after his wife, an American pianist, left him. Hans Morgenthau was supposed to visit Arendt in Tegna, but suffered a stroke, and the German writer Uwe Johnson, who had intended to come at the end of her trip, had a coronary. Despite the onslaught of bad news and her sadness about Heidegger, Arendt assures McCarthy it was a beautiful summer.[10]

But this time when Hannah Arendt returned to 370 Riverside Drive she found it difficult to go out into the world. She spent her days at home in routine working on *The Life of the Mind*. Guests came to her in the evenings, and there was a celebration with the tribe on the occasion of her 69th birthday, but Arendt had grown tired of New York. The day after Thanksgiving, she tripped on a pothole and fell into the street. Passersby gathered around her, while a policeman was summoned, but Arendt was able to pick herself up and make it inside the building before he arrived. She did not tell anyone about the fall, and lied to Mary McCarthy about making a doctor's appointment. When she finally did make one, she didn't keep it.

A few weeks later, on Thursday 4 December, Arendt invited Salo and Jeanette Baron for dinner at 8:00 p.m. After their meal, they retired to Arendt's living room where she served them coffee. While they were talking, Arendt suffered a brief coughing spell, sank into her chair and lost consciousness. Salo and Jeanette found a medicine bottle in a cabinet and called her doctor. When the doctor arrived he summoned Lotte Köhler, but by the time Lotte arrived it was too late. Hannah Arendt had died from a massive heart attack.

As Lotte had done for Blücher, she sent a telegram to their tribe, letting them know Hannah was gone. The next day her research assistant Larry May found the title page for the third volume of *The Life of the Mind* in her typewriter. It contained the title 'Judging' and two epigraphs. The first was about Cato from Lucan's *Pharsalia*, 'Victrix causa diis placuit sed victa Catoni' (The victorious cause pleased the gods, but the defeated one pleased Cato), with which Arendt had concluded the *Postscriptum* to 'Thinking'. The second was from Part II, Act V, of Goethe's *Faust*:

If I could remove the magic from my path,
And utterly forget all enchanted spells,
Nature, I would stand before you as but a man,
Then it would be worth the effort of being a man.

A memorial service was held for Hannah Arendt in the Riverside Memorial Chapel on Amsterdam Avenue and 76th Street in New York on 8 December 1975. Her funeral was a simple affair. She was placed in a pine coffin covered with white roses. The night before the service, her friends debated whether or not the Jewish prayers should be said. The conclusion was a compromise: Arendt's niece read a psalm in Hebrew and Daniel Klenbort, Chanan's Klenbort's son, read it in English.

Some three hundred mourners congregated to remember Hannah Arendt. Jerome Kohn, Arendt's last teaching assistant at the New School for Social Research, described her as 'one of the great teachers of our times'. Hans Jonas spoke about her passion for life: 'Things looked different after she looked at them.' Arendt's publisher, William Jovanovich, said,

Hannah Arendt in Marbach, Germany, 1975.

She was passionate in the way believers in justice can become and that believers in mercy must remain. She detested violence but defended disobedience in a just civil cause. She followed wherever serious inquiry would take her, and if she made enemies it was never out of fear. As for me, I loved her fiercely ... Hannah made me less embarrassed to be human.[11]

Mary McCarthy described Arendt as 'a physical being':

She was a beautiful woman, alluring, seductive; most speakingly the eyes, which were brilliant, sparkling as though rays of intelligence leaped out of them, but also deep dark pools of inwardness. There was something unfathomable in Hannah that seemed to lie in the reflective depths of those eyes.[12]

The following month, McCarthy's tribute was published in the *New York Review of Books*:

> In her coffin, with the lids veiling the fathomless eyes, that noble forehead topped by a sort of pompadour, she was not Hannah any more but a composed death mask of an eighteenth-century philosopher. I was not moved to touch that grand stranger in the funeral parlor, and only in the soft yet roughened furrows of her neck, in which the public head rested, could I find a place to tell her good-bye.[13]

That spring Hannah Arendt's ashes were buried next to Heinrich Blücher's in the Bard College cemetery in Annandale-on-Hudson, New York. And after everything, amidst the praise and consolations offered in this realm of human affairs, Hannah Arendt had achieved that rare heroic feat she described so elegantly in *The Human Condition*: immortality.

20

Storytelling

In Greek and Roman mythology, Pheme, or Fama, was given
the power to bestow immortal fame and destroy reputations by
spreading half-truths and lies. Because of these twin powers, the
goddess of Fame is portrayed as good and evil. The poet Hesiod
described her as an evil-doer. Virgil portrayed her as a swift,
birdlike monster, with eyes, lips, tongues and ears at the tips of her
feathers raking the ground while her head soars through the clouds.
According to Ovid, she dwells in a mountain-top palace of echoing
brass. She favours the notable and scorns those who defy her by
plaguing them with rumours. Daughter of Earth, it is said that as
Fama learns of the affairs of mortal men she begins to whisper
them quietly until her voice grows so loud the whole world can hear.

But as Hannah Arendt recognized, fame is a social
phenomenon. People never get to tell their own story, and one can
never predict who Fama will bless or curse. It happens that Hannah
Arendt's legacy has been touched by both of Fama's powers. During
her time she was confronted by no shortage of rumours and half-
truths about her life and work, but she also has posthumously
gained immortal fame.

It would be misleading to say Hannah Arendt was a
philosopher or a political theorist. To describe her work, one
would be better equipped with a list of paradoxes: Hannah
Arendt was a poetic thinker without being a poet, though she
wrote poetry. Hannah Arendt was not a philosopher, though she

engaged in the work of philosophy. Hannah Arendt was not a biographer, though she wrote many biographical texts in order to better understand the human condition. Hannah Arendt was not a journalist, critic, essayist, book reviewer, editor or political activist, though she gave a part of herself to each of these activities as they appeared before her. Perhaps, if we demanded a positive claim, we might say with Mary McCarthy that Hannah Arendt has joined the ranks of Socrates and Karl Jaspers as the embodiment of a thinker par excellence. But I suspect she might have rejected this, too.

Jerome Kohn once noted, 'The problem with Hannah Arendt was that she knew too much.' One can imagine this 'knew' in two senses: as the acquisition of learnedness, and in the relational sense of developing a connection. What separated and continues to separate Arendt's work from others is the ways in which she was able to make connections across bodies of literature that she read and memorized. Liberated from tradition, Arendt was free to see the world anew, and in doing so, confront the experiences of her generation. Her command of poetry, philosophy, politics and literature gave her a sense of durability in a world plagued by uncertainty. The metaphor she used for thinking was 'thinking without a banister'. She described this thinking as wandering endlessly up and down a staircase with nothing to hold on to. There might not be anything to hold to, but Arendt's metaphor does give one something to stand on – those steps she was free to roam were the inheritance left to her by no testament.

Arendt never defined who she was: she understood that who one is is not something they alone get to decide. Who we are can only be revealed through our words and deeds in the public realm of human affairs. What we are is a fact of our existence and conditions our experiences in the world, but it does not determine our fate. The one time Hannah Arendt claimed her identity was when she felt it was politically necessary as a Jewish refugee. Zionism, as she saw it, was the only solution to the Jewish problem in those days. And her Zionism was a reflection of the lesson her mother had taught her as a small child: 'When one is attacked as a Jew, one must defend oneself as a Jew.'

But Arendt knew no love of a people, and she resisted the ideological impulse of such a notion. To be born a woman, to be born a Jew, were, much like fame, something she had no control over. These were facts of her appearance in the world. When Gershom Scholem told her she had no love of her people, she could not deny his accusation. To demand such love is to demand a kind of blindness that turns one away from the world of experience. What is ironic about Arendt's position, though, is that one must love a person or people very much to critique and judge them the way she did. This is what she meant by love of the world. One cannot take the good while turning a blind eye to the bad. Arendt rejected the claim that her identity ought to make her think or act in a certain way. It is clear from even a brief perusal of her life that nobody told her how to think or act, ever. When she was invited to participate in a discussion with the historian Howard Sachar, who had publicly decried her work, she responded with her usual flair stating: 'I hate to be so difficult, but I'm afraid the truth is I am.'

Since the early 1980s, with the publication of Elisabeth Young-Bruehl's sweeping biography *Hannah Arendt: For Love of the World*, countless volumes of posthumous work and correspondence have been published, giving readers an even fuller picture of Arendt's life and work. And not surprisingly the unearthed documents and translated texts have only fuelled Fama's Janus-faced judgement. Arendt's reportage on *Eichmann in Jerusalem* perennially flashes up as a site of debate, and provides no shortage of newcomers with fuel to inspire and infuriate. And so to Arendt's relationship with Martin Heidegger, which continues to produce some of the best and worst reflective essays. More recently a body of scholarship has appeared dealing with the question of Hannah Arendt and race.

In the past few years, with the rise of illiberalism worldwide, Hannah Arendt's work on *The Origins of Totalitarianism* has garnered unprecedented attention. Richard Bernstein has written an accessible book on *Why Read Hannah Arendt Now?*, and endless essays have been penned around the world about Arendt's analysis of fascism and totalitarianism. While her work can help orient us to our present moment, as we face a new century defined by new phenomena, we must come face-to-face with what is in front of us. Our century is not Hannah Arendt's, and this is part of Arendt's challenge to us. At the heart of her work is the argument that we must continuously think the world anew, define new limits, draw new constellations, find new language and tell new stories. This is the inheritance she has left us.

And one can almost see Hannah Arendt standing over her wooden desk, in front of her blue typewriter, with enormous silver scissors and a roll of Scotch tape in her hand, making an image as much as a text, alive with the desire for understanding.

References

Introduction: Understanding

1   Emily Dickinson, *The Complete Poems of Emily Dickinson*, ed. Thomas H. Johnson (Cambridge, MA, 1960), p. 151 (poem 320).

2   Hannah Arendt, *The Human Condition* (Chicago, IL, 1998), p. 5.

3   Carol Brightman, ed., *Between Friends: The Correspondence of Hannah Arendt and Mary McCarthy, 1949–1975* (New York, 1995), p. 391.

4   Hans Jonas, quoted in Elisabeth Young-Bruehl, *Hannah Arendt: For Love of the World* (New Haven, CT, 2004), p. 18.

5   Julia Kristeva and Frank Collins, *Hannah Arendt: Life Is a Narrative* (Toronto, 2001), p. 25.

6   Lionel Abel, quoted in Daniel Maier-Katkin, 'The Reception of Hannah Arendt's *Eichmann in Jerusalem* in the United States, 1963–2011', VI/1–2 (2011), www.hannaharendt.net, accessed 28 July 2020.

7   Office Memorandum, U.S. Government. Letter to FBI Director, 30 April 1956.

8   'Zur Person', ZDF, 28 October 1964; transcribed as Hannah Arendt, 'What Remains? Language Remains: A Conversation with Günter Gaus', trans. Joan Stambaugh, in *Essays in Understanding, 1930–1954*, ed. Jerome Kohn (New York, 1994), pp. 1–23. Arendt said, 'What is important for me is to understand.'

9   Hannah Arendt, *The Portable Hannah Arendt*, trans. Joan Stambaugh, ed. Peter Baehr (New York, 2003), p. 11.

10 Hannah Arendt, *Denktagebuch. Bd. 1: 1950–1973*, ed. Ursula Ludz and Ingrid Nordmann (Zürich, 2002).

11 Hannah Arendt, *The Life of the Mind*, ed. Mary McCarthy (New York, 1981), p. 176.

12 Hannah Arendt, 'Understanding and Politics (The Difficulties of Understanding)', in *Essays in Understanding, 1930–1954*, ed. Jerome Kohn (New York, 1994), pp. 307–27.

13 Hannah Arendt's correspondence with Roger Errera is held in the Hannah Arendt Archive in the Library of Congress, Washington, DC.

14 I thank my Bard College colleague Thomas Wild for this insight.

15 Hannah Arendt, 'Zionism Reconsidered', in *The Jewish Writings*, ed. Jerome Kohn and Ron H. Feldman (New York, 2007), p. 374.

1 Inner Awakening

1 Hannah Arendt, 'Preface to the First Edition', *The Origins of Totalitarianism* (London, 2017), p. iii.

2 Elisabeth Young-Bruehl, *Hannah Arendt: For Love of the World* (New Haven, CT, 1982), p. 13.

3 David Sorkin, 'Wilhelm von Humboldt: The Theory and Practice of Self-Formation (*Bildung*), 1791–1810', *Journal of the History of Ideas*, XLIV/1 (1983), pp. 55–73.

4 Author's translation. Martha Arendt, 'Notre enfant', in Hannah Arendt, À *travers le mur: un conte et trois paraboles*, ed. Karin Biro (Paris, 2017), p. 56.

5 Ibid., pp. 55–6.

6 Young-Bruehl, *Hannah Arendt*, p. 10.

7 Hannah Arendt, *The Portable Hannah Arendt*, trans. Joan Stambaugh, ed. Peter Baehr (New York, 2003), pp. 7–8; Young-Bruehl recounts the event: 'Hannah Arendt came home from her elementary school one day to ask her mother if what one of her schoolmates had told her was true – that her grandfather had murdered the Lord Jesus'; *Hannah Arendt*, p. 11.

8 Max Arendt married Johanna Wohlgemuth and had Arendt's father Paul and another child. When Johanna died he married her sister, Klara.

9 After the Battle of Tannenberg at the end of August, followed by Field Marshal von Hindenburg's defeat of the Russians at the First Battle of the Masurian Lakes, the Russians were forced to retreat completely from East Prussia.

10 'Zur Person', ZDF, 28 October 1964; transcribed as Hannah Arendt, 'What Remains? Language Remains: A Conversation with Günter Gaus', trans. Joan Stambaugh, in *Essays in Understanding, 1930–1954*, ed. Jerome Kohn (New York, 1994), pp. 1–23.

11 Young-Bruehl, *Hannah Arendt: For Love of the World*, p. 33.

12 Ibid., p. 29.

2 Shadows

1 Author's translation. Hannah Arendt, *Denktagebuch*, I, Notebook 4, Entry 13, p. 91.
2 Antonia Grunenberg, *Hannah Arendt and Martin Heidegger: History of a Love* (Bloomington, IN, 2017), p. 17.
3 Hans-Georg Gadamer, quoted ibid., p. 58.
4 Hannah Arendt and Martin Heidegger, *Letters, 1925–1975*, ed. Ursula Ludz, trans. Andrew Shields (New York, 2004), p. 9.
5 Ibid., p. 3.
6 Ibid., p. 50.
7 Ibid., pp. 12–13.
8 Both copies are in Hannah Arendt's Archive at the Library of Congress in Washington, DC.
9 Arendt and Heidegger, *Letters*, pp. 52–3.
10 Hannah Arendt, 'Heidegger the Fox', in *Essays in Understanding, 1930–1954*, ed. Jerome Kohn (New York, 1994), pp. 361–2.
11 Hannah Arendt to Karl Jaspers, 9 July 1946, in Hannah Arendt and Karl Jaspers, *Correspondence, 1926–1969*, ed. Lotte Köhler and Hans Saner, trans. Robert and Rita Kimber (New York, 1992).
12 In 2014 Heidegger's *Black Notebooks* were published. The *Notebooks* bring together more than a thousand pages of carefully detailed entries that Heidegger wrote between the early 1930s and late 1970s, and reveal a conscious awareness of National Socialism, suggesting that his participation was not unthinking. In particular the *Notebooks* contain several explicit anti-Semitic passages that address the way he thought about the Jewish people and world history. Hannah Arendt never saw Heidegger's *Notebooks*, so it would be pure speculation to imagine what she would have thought if she had read them.

3 Love and Saint Augustine

1 Elisabeth Young-Bruehl, *Hannah Arendt: For Love of the World* (New Haven, CT, 1982), p. 64.
2 Joanna Vecchiarelli Scott and Judith Chelius Stark, 'Rediscovering Love and Saint Augustine', preface to Hannah Arendt, *Love and Saint*

Augustine, ed. Scott and Stark (Chicago, IL, 1996), p. xv.
3 Ibid., p. 76.
4 Hannah Arendt, *The Origins of Totalitarianism* (New York, 1973), p. 479.

4 Life of a Jewess

1 This is an abridged summary of Hitler's rise to power for historical context. If you are looking for a more detailed timeline, I would suggest that given on the website of the United States Holocaust Memorial Museum (www.ushmm.org).
2 Sybille Bedford, 'Emancipation and Destiny', *Book News*, 12 December 1958; quoted in Elisabeth Young-Bruehl, *Hannah Arendt: For Love of the World* (New Haven, CT, 1982), p. 87.
3 Ibid., p. 197.
4 Ibid., p. 196.
5 Ibid.
6 Hannah Arendt and Martin Heidegger, *Letters, 1925–1975*, ed. Ursula Ludz, trans. Andrew Shields (New York, 2004), pp. 37–8.
7 Author's translation. Günther Anders, *Die Kirschenschlacht: Dialoge mit Hannah* (Munich, 2011).
8 Ibid., pp. 11–12.
9 Young-Bruehl, *Hannah Arendt*, p. 79.
10 Jason Dawsey, *History after Hiroshima: Günther Anders and the Twentieth Century*, September 2004, www.marcuse.faculty.history.ucsb.edu, accessed 31 July 2020.
11 Young-Bruehl, *Hannah Arendt*, p. 134.
12 www.guenther-anders-gesellschaft.org/vita-english.
13 Despite these distinct differences there are many overlapping grounds of interest where they might have met in conversation, particularly around Kantian judgement. Arendt and Adorno both employed critique in their work in the Kantian sense of analysing the conditions, possibilities and limits of rational faculties in reasoning itself, assuming a self-reflective position for understanding the world.
14 Young-Bruehl, *Hannah Arendt*, p. 84.
15 Hannah Arendt, 'On the Emancipation of Women', in *Essays in Understanding, 1930–1954*, ed. Jerome Kohn (New York, 1994), pp. 67–8.

16 Hannah Arendt, 'Rosa Luxemburg', in *Men in Dark Times* (New York, 1968), p. 44.

5 Turn Towards Politics

1 Hannah Arendt, 'What Remains? Language Remains: A Conversation with Günter Gaus', trans. Joan Stambaugh, in *Essays in Understanding, 1930–1954*, ed. Jerome Kohn (New York, 1994), pp. 4–5.
2 Hannah Arendt, 'The Image of Hell', ibid., p. 203.
3 Hannah Arendt, 'What Remains?', p. 12.
4 Elisabeth Young-Bruehl, *Hannah Arendt: For Love of the World* (New Haven, CT, 1982), p. 106.
5 Ibid., pp. 5–6.
6 Young-Bruehl, *Hannah Arendt*, p. 106.
7 Ibid., p. 107.

6 'We Refugees'

1 Elisabeth Young-Bruehl, *Hannah Arendt: For Love of the World* (New Haven, CT, 1982), p. 119.
2 Ibid., p. 116.
3 Michael S. Roth, 'A Problem of Recognition: Alexandre Kojève and the End of History', *History and Theory*, XXIV/3 (1985), pp. 293–306.
4 Hannah Arendt's application to the Emergency Committee in Aid of Displaced Foreign Scholars is held at the New York Public Library in the Manuscript Division.
5 Young-Bruehl, *Hannah Arendt*, p. 120.
6 Hannah Arendt, 'We Refugees', in *The Jewish Writings*, ed. Jerome Kohn and Ron H. Feldman (New York, 2007), p. 272.
7 Ibid., p. 271.
8 Hannah Arendt, 'Some Young People Are Going Home', in *The Jewish Writings*, p. 34.
9 Carol Brightman, ed., *Between Friends: The Correspondence of Hannah Arendt and Mary McCarthy, 1949–1975* (New York, 1996), p. 248.
10 Young-Bruehl, *Hannah Arendt*, p. 134.

11   Hannah Arendt and Martin Heidegger, *Letters, 1925–1975*, ed. Ursula Ludz, trans. Andrew Shields (New York, 2004), p. 61.

12   'August 24, 1936', ibid.

13   Hannah Arendt's family papers are located in the Hannah Arendt archive at the Library of Congress in Washington, DC.

14   Young-Bruehl, *Hannah Arendt*, p. 135.

15   Ibid.

16   Ibid., p. 133.

17   Hannah Arendt and Heinrich Blücher, 'Geneva, September 18, 1937', in *Within Four Walls: The Correspondence between Hannah Arendt and Heinrich Blücher, 1936–1968*, ed. Lotte Köhler (New York, 2000), pp. 40–41.

7 Internment

1   Howard Eiland and Michael W. Jennings, *Walter Benjamin: A Critical Life* (Cambridge, MA, 2014), pp. 648–9.

2   Hannah Arendt, *Men in Dark Times* (New York, 1968), p. 245.

3   Ibid.

4   Lisa Fittko, *Escape through the Pyrenees* (Evanston, IL, 2000), p. 10.

5   This account is a synopsis of ibid. and research done on the Jewish Virtual Library's website: www.jewishvirtual.org.

6   Hanna Schramm and Barbara Vormeier, *Vivre à Gurs: un camp de concentration français, 1940–1941* (Paris, 1979).

7   Frederick Raymes and Menachem Mayer, *Are the Trees in Bloom Over There?* (Jerusalem, 2002), pp. 79–82.

8   'Gurs Transit Camp', www.jewishvirtuallibrary.org, accessed December 2019.

9   Hannah Arendt, 'We Refugees', in *The Jewish Writings* (New York, 2007), pp. 267–8.

10   Tadeusz Borowski, *This Way for the Gas, Ladies and Gentlemen* (1967) (New York, 1992), p. 122.

11   Elisabeth Young-Bruehl, *Hannah Arendt: For Love of the World* (New Haven, CT, 1982), p. 154.

12   Bruno Bettelheim, 'Freedom from Ghetto Thinking', *Midstream* (Spring 1962), pp. 16–25.

13   Fittko, *Escape through the Pyrenees*, p. 43.

8 State of Emergency

1 Lisa Fittko, *Escape through the Pyrenees* (Evanston, IL, 2000), p. 66.
2 Marie Luise Knott, ed., *The Correspondence of Hannah Arendt and Gershom Scholem*, trans. Anthony David (Chicago, IL, 2017), p. 7.
3 'At the beginning of July, I left Lourdes *à la recherche de mon mari perdu* [looking for my lost husband]. Benji was hardly thrilled, and I vacillated back and forth if I should take him with me. But that would have been simply impossible.' Ibid., p. 8.
4 Elisabeth Young-Bruehl, *Hannah Arendt: For Love of the World* (New Haven, CT, 1982), p. 156.
5 Lyndsey Stonebridge, 'Why Hannah Arendt is the philosopher for now', *New Statesman* (20 March 2019).
6 John Vinocur, 'Varian Fry Fought U.S. State Dept. to Rescue Jews in World War II: Marseille Honors an American Hero', *New York Times*, 19 October 2020.
7 Young-Bruehl, *Hannah Arendt*, pp. 158–9.
8 Walter Benjamin, *Theses on the Philosophy of History* (New York, 1968), p. 257.
9 Hannah Arendt, introduction to Walter Benjamin, *Illuminations* (New York, 1968), p. 5.

9 Transition

1 Hannah Arendt and Günther Anders, *Schreib doch mal 'hard facts' über Dich: Briefe, 1939 bis 1975*, ed. Kerstin Putz (Munich, 2018), p. 23.
2 Elisabeth Young-Bruehl, *Hannah Arendt: For Love of the World* (New Haven, CT, 1982), p. 164.
3 Lotte Köhler, ed., *Within Four Walls: The Correspondence between Hannah Arendt and Heinrich Blücher, 1936–1968* (New York, 2000), p. 59.
4 Ibid., p. 60.
5 Ibid.
6 Hans Jonas, 'Hannah Arendt: An Intimate Portrait', *New England Review*, XXVII/2 (2006), pp. 133–42.

7　Hannah Arendt, 'Is America by Nature a Violent Society?', in *Thinking Without a Banister: Essays in Understanding, 1953–1975*, ed. Jerome Kohn (New York, 2018), p. 355.

8　Köhler, ed., *Within Four Walls*, p. 63.

9　Salo W. Baron, 'Hannah Arendt (1906–1975)', *Jewish Social Studies*, XXXVIII/2 (1976), pp. 187–9.

10　Hannah Arendt, *The Jewish Writings* (New York, 2007), p. 163.

11　Young-Bruehl, *Hannah Arendt*, p. 177.

12　Ibid., p. 181.

13　Hannah Arendt, *The Origins of Totalitarianism* (New York, 1951), p. 56.

14　Elisabeth Young-Bruehl, *Hannah Arendt*, p. 174.

10 Friendship

1　Hannah Arendt to Karl Jaspers, in Hannah Arendt and Karl Jaspers, *Correspondence, 1926–1969*, ed. Lotte Köhler and Hans Saner, trans. Robert and Rita Kimber (New York, 1992), p. 23.

2　Ibid., p. 24.

3　Kathleen B. Jones, 'Hannah Arendt's Female Friends', *Los Angeles Review of Books* (12 November 2013).

4　Ibid.

5　*Politics*, stylized as *politics*, was a journal founded and edited by Dwight Macdonald from 1944 to 1949. Macdonald had previously been editor at *Partisan Review* from 1937 to 1943, but after falling out with its publishers, quit to start *politics* as a rival publication, first on a monthly basis and then as a quarterly.

6　Hannah Arendt, *Thinking Without a Banister: Essays in Understanding, 1953–1975*, ed. Jerome Kohn (New York, 2018).

7　Hannah Arendt, *Men in Dark Times* (New York, 1968), p. 263.

8　Ibid., p. 264.

9　Quoted in Elisabeth Young-Bruehl, *Hannah Arendt: For Love of the World* (New Haven, CT, 1982), p. 192.

10　Ibid., p. 190.

11　Hannah Ahrendt, 'Franz Kafka: A Reevaluation', *Partisan Review*, XI/4 (1944).

12　*Die Wandlumg*, 1/12 (1945–6); *Sechs Essays* (Heidelberg, 1948), rev. as *Die verborgene Tradition: Acht Essays* (Frankfurt, 1976).

13 Hannah Arendt, *Reflections on Literature and Culture*, ed. Susannah Gottlieb (Stanford, CA, 2007), p. 122.

14 These telegrams are located in the Hannah Arendt archive at the Library of Congress in Washington, DC, in Arendt's correspondence with Eva Beerwald.

15 Lotte Köhler, ed., *Within Four Walls: The Correspondence between Hannah Arendt and Heinrich Blücher, 1936–1968* (New York, 2000).

11 Reconciliation

1 Salo W. Baron, 'Hannah Arendt (1906–1975)', *Jewish Social Studies*, XXXVIII/2 (1976), pp. 187–9.

2 Lotte Köhler, ed., *Within Four Walls: The Correspondence between Hannah Arendt and Heinrich Blücher, 1936–1968* (New York, 2000), p. 115. In a letter dated 5 February 1950 Hannah writes to Heinrich: 'In Heidelberg I heard an absolutely outrageous story of what Heidegger has done to Jaspers, now that he is trying, trying as hard as possible, to make friends on the other side. Will be in Freiburg on Monday, will have to be, but no longer have the slightest wish ever to see that man again. Jaspers knows nothing. Should I tell him? Should I maybe not? I don't know. I'm at a loss.'

3 Hans Jonas, 'Hannah Arendt: An Intimate Portrait', *New England Review*, XXVII/2 (2006), pp. 133–42.

4 Elzbieta Ettinger, *Hannah Arendt/Martin Heidegger* (New Haven, CT, 1997), p. 70.

5 Köhler, ed., *Within Four Walls*, p. 59.

6 Ibid.

7 Ibid., p. 123.

12 *The Origins of Totalitarianism*

1 Hannah Arendt and Karl Jaspers, *Correspondence, 1926–1969*, ed. Lotte Köhler and Hans Saner (New York, 1993), p. 34.

2 Hannah Arendt, 'Race-Thinking before Racism', *Review of Politics*, VI/1 (1944), pp. 36–73.

3 Hannah Arendt, *The Origins of Totalitarianism* (New York, 1951), p. 444.
4 Peter Baehr and Gordon C. Wells, 'Debating Totalitarianism: An Exchange of Letters between Hannah Arendt and Eric Voegelin', *History and Theory*, LI/3 (2012), pp. 364–80.
5 Hannah Arendt, 'Totalitarianism', in *The Portable Hannah Arendt*, trans. Joan Stambaugh, ed. Peter Baehr (New York, 2003), pp. 77–8.
6 Arendt, *The Origins of Totalitarianism*, p. 138.
7 Elisabeth Young-Bruehl, *Hannah Arendt: For Love of the World* (New Haven, CT, 1982), p. 276.
8 Ibid., p. 263.
9 Author's translation. Hannah Arendt, *Denktagebuch*, I, Notebook 8, Entry 30, p. 197.
10 Hannah Arendt, 'The Ex-Communists', *The Commonweal* (20 March 1953), pp. 595–9; cited in Jerome Kohn, 'Hannah Arendt – Among Friends?', Hannah Arendt Center for Politics and Humanities, 3 December 2015, https://hac.bard.edu, accessed 6 August 2020.
11 *Yale Daily News*, 8 November 1968; Hannah Arendt Archive, Library of Congress, Clippings, 1941–1975.
12 Young-Bruehl, *Hannah Arendt*, p. 270.

13 *Amor Mundi*

1 Hannah Arendt, *The Human Condition* (Chicago, IL, 1958), p. 1.
2 Ibid., pp. 7–8.
3 Ibid., p. 9.
4 Hannah Arendt, *On Revolution* (New York, 1963), p. 275.
5 Hannah Arendt, 'Karl Marx and the Tradition of Western Political Thought', *Social Research*, LXIX/2 (2002), pp. 273–319.
6 Hannah Arendt and Karl Jaspers, *Correspondence, 1926–1969*, ed. Lotte Köhler and Hans Saner (New York, 1993), p. 160.
7 Ibid., p. 163.
8 Ibid., p. 167.
9 Arendt, *The Human Condition*, p. 256.
10 Ibid., p. 5.
11 Hannah Arendt, *Denktagebuch*, Notebook 21, Section 68, August, 1955: 'Heidegger hat unrecht: "in die Welt" ist der Mensch nicht "geworfen";

wenn wir geworfen sind, so – nicht anders als die Tiere – auf die Erde. In die Welt gerade wird der Mensch geleitet, nicht geworfen, da gerade stellt sich seine Kontinuität her und offenbart seine Zugehörigkeit. Wehe uns, wenn wir in die Welt geworfen werden!' ('Heidegger is wrong: man is not "thrown" "in the world"; if we are thrown, then – no differently from animals – onto the earth. Man is precisely guided, not thrown, precisely for that reason his continuity arises and the way he belongs appears. Poor us, if we are thrown into the world!')

12 Hannah Arendt and Martin Heidegger, *Letters, 1925–1975*, ed. Ursula Ludz, trans. Andrew Shields (New York, 2004), pp. 123–4.

14 *Between Past and Future*

1 Elisabeth Young-Bruehl, *Hannah Arendt: For Love of the World* (New Haven, CT, 1982), p. 235.

2 Hannah Arendt, *Between Past and Future* (New York, 1961), p. 8.

3 Ibid., p. 14.

4 Hannah Arendt and Karl Jaspers, *Correspondence, 1926–1969*, ed. Lotte Köhler and Hans Saner (New York, 1993), p. 385.

5 Ibid.

6 Ibid., p. 386.

7 Hannah Arendt, 'Reflections on Little Rock', *Dissent*, VI/1 (Winter 1959), pp. 45–56.

8 Robert Penn Warren, *Who Speaks for the Negro?* [1965] (New Haven, CT, 2014), pp. 343–4.

9 Letter to Ralph Ellison, 29 July 1965. Correspondence, Miscellaneous, E, The Hannah Arendt Papers at the Library of Congress, http://memory.loc.gov, accessed 8 August 2020. In recent years scholars have begun to address the racialized language in Hannah Arendt's writing.

15 *Eichmann in Jerusalem*

1 Saskia Hamilton, ed., *The Letters of Robert Lowell* (New York, 2005), p. 760.

2 Jerome Kohn, 'Evil: The Crime against Humanity', in 'Three Essays: The Role of Experience in Hannah Arendt's Political Thought', *The Hannah Arendt Papers at the Library of Congress*, https://memory.loc. gov, accessed 8 August 2020.

3 Elisabeth Young-Bruehl, *Hannah Arendt: For Love of the World* (New Haven, CT, 1982), p. 329.

4 Lotte Köhler, ed., *Within Four Walls: The Correspondence between Hannah Arendt and Heinrich Blücher, 1936–1968* (New York, 2000), p. 357.

5 Ibid., p. 364.

6 Ibid., p. 363.

7 Hannah Arendt, *Eichmann in Jerusalem: A Report on the Banality of Evil* (New York, 1963).

8 Marie Luise Knott, ed., 'Letter 132, June 23, 1963', in *The Correspondence of Hannah Arendt and Gershom Scholem*, trans. Anthony David (Chicago, IL, 2017).

9 'Letter 133, July 20, 1963', ibid.

10 Hannah Arendt, letter to James Baldwin, 21 November 1962, Library of Congress Archive, 005041.

11 Knott, ed., *The Correspondence of Hannah Arendt and Gershom Scholem*, p. 209.

12 Hannah Arendt, *Thinking Without a Banister: Essays in Understanding, 1953–1975*, ed. Jerome Kohn (New York, 2018), pp. 278–9.

13 Hannah Arendt, draft of letter to Samuel Grafton, *The Hannah Arendt Papers at the Library of Congress*, https://memory.loc.gov, accessed 8 August 2020.

14 Young-Bruehl, *Hannah Arendt*, p. 334.

15 Carol Brightman, ed., *Between Friends: The Correspondence of Hannah Arendt and Mary McCarthy, 1949–1975* (New York, 1996), p. 124.

16 Ibid., pp. 126–7.

17 Arendt was awarded an insurance settlement for her 1962 automobile accident, when her taxi was struck by a New York City motor vehicle. The settlement award subsidized a vacation that Arendt, Heinrich Blücher and Charlotte Beradt took to Greece.

16 *On Revolution*

1 Elisabeth Young-Bruehl, *Hannah Arendt: For Love of the World* (New Haven, CT, 1982), p. 385.
2 Hannah Arendt, *Thinking Without a Banister: Essays in Understanding, 1953–1975*, ed. Jerome Kohn (New York, 2018), p. 192.
3 Eugene Wolters, 'When Fidel Castro Met Hannah Arendt', *Critical Theory*, 17 September 2014, www.critical-theory.com, accessed 8 August 2020.
4 Hannah Arendt, 'What Freedom and Revolution Really Means, Thoughts on Poverty, Misery, and the Great Revolutions of History', *New England Review*, XXXVIII/2 (2017), available at https://lithub.com, accessed 6 August 2020.
5 Hannah Arendt, 'Revolutions Spurious and Genuine' (1964), *HannahArendt.net*, 1/7 (November 2013), www.hannaharendt.net, accessed 8 August 2020.
6 Hannah Arendt, 'The Great Tradition', *Thinking Without a Banister*, p. 52.
7 Young-Bruehl, *Hannah Arendt*, pp. 397–8.
8 Ibid, p. 398.
9 Hannah Arendt, 'Truth and Politics', *New Yorker* (25 February 1967), p. 49.
10 Ibid.
11 Ibid.
12 Ibid.

17 *Men in Dark Times*

1 Elisabeth Young-Bruehl, *Hannah Arendt: For Love of the World* (New Haven, CT, 1982), p. 396.
2 Hannah Arendt, 'Bertolt Brecht, 1898–1956', *Men in Dark Times* (New York, 1968), pp. 207–50.
3 For further reading see Jerome Kohn, 'Hannah Arendt's Judgment of Bertolt Brecht', *Social Research*, LXXXVI/3 (Fall 2019), pp. 651–69.
4 Young-Bruehl, *Hannah Arendt*, p. 390.
5 I offer a detailed account of Hannah Arendt's publication of Benjamin's final work in Samantha Rose Hill, 'Walter Benjamin's Last Work', *Los Angeles Review of Books*, 9 December 2019, https://lareviewofbooks.org.
6 Arendt, *Men in Dark Times*, p. vii.

7 Quoted in Carol Brightman, ed., *Between Friends: The Correspondence of Hannah Arendt and Mary McCarthy, 1949–1975* (New York, 1996), p. 225.

8 Ibid., pp. 225–32.

9 Lotte Köhler, ed., *Within Four Walls: The Correspondence between Hannah Arendt and Heinrich Blücher, 1936–1968* (New York, 2000), p. 388.

10 Young-Bruehl, *Hannah Arendt*, p. 423.

18 *Crises of the Republic*

1 This text was never published, but a transcript can be found in Hannah Arendt's archive at the Library of Congress in Washington, DC, and digitally at https://memory.loc.gov.

2 Elisabeth Young-Bruehl, *Hannah Arendt: For Love of the World* (New Haven, CT, 1982), p. 414.

3 Ibid.

4 Ibid., p. 268. Blücher's words are from a letter to his mother, Klara Blücher, April 1946, Library of Congress.

5 Ibid., p. 436.

19 *The Life of the Mind*

1 Hannah Arendt, 'Thinking and Moral Considerations', *Social Research*, XXXVIII/3 (1971), p. 438.

2 Ibid., p. 436.

3 Carol Brightman, ed., *Between Friends: The Correspondence of Hannah Arendt and Mary McCarthy, 1949–1975* (New York, 1996), p. 201.

4 Elisabeth Young-Bruehl, *Hannah Arendt: For Love of the World* (New Haven, CT, 1982), p. 447.

5 Ibid. This is a summary of Young-Bruehl's account.

6 Ibid., p. 436.

7 Hannah Arendt, 'Remembering Wystan H. Auden, Who Died in the Night of the Twenty-eighth of September, 1973', *New Yorker* (20 January 1975); repr. in *Reflections on Literature and Culture*, ed. Susannah Young-Ah Gottlieb (Stanford, CA, 2007), pp. 294–302.

8 Barry Gewen, 'Hans Morgenthau and Hannah Arendt: An Intellectual Passion', www.nationalinterest.org, 25 August 2015.

9 Hans Morgenthau to Hannah Arendt, Hannah Arendt Archive at the Library of Congress, Washington, DC.

10 Brightman, ed., *Between Friends*, pp. 385–6.

11 David Bird, 'Hannah Arendt's Funeral Held: Many Moving Tributes Paid', *New York Times*, 9 December 1975.

12 Ibid.

13 Mary McCarthy, 'Saying Good-bye to Hannah', *New York Review of Books* (22 January 1976).

Select Bibliography

Writings

Der Liebesbegriff bei Augustin (Berlin, 1929); trans. as *Love and Saint Augustine*, ed. Joanna Vecchiarelli and Judith Chelius Stark (Chicago, IL, 1996)

Sechs Essays (Heidelberg, 1948); rev. as *Die verborgene Tradition: Acht Essays*

The Origins of Totalitarianism (New York, 1951); as *The Burden of Our Time* (London, 1951); trans. as *Elemente und Ursprünge totaler Herrschaft* (Frankfurt, 1955)

Fragwürdige Traditionsbestände im politischen Denken der Gegenwart (Frankfurt, 1957); trans. in *Between Past and Future: Six Exercises in Political Thought* (New York, 1961)

The Human Condition (Chicago, IL, 1958); trans. as *Vita activa oder von tätigen Leben* (Stuttgart, 1960)

Rahel Varnhagen: The Life of a Jewess (London, 1958); trans. as *Rahel Varnhagen: Lebensgeschichte einer deutschen Jüdin aus der Romantik* (Munich, 1959); U.S. edn as *Rahel Varnhagen: The Life of a Jewish Woman* (New York, 1974)

Die Ungarische Revolution und der totalitäre Imperialismus (Munich, 1958); trans. in *The Origins of Totalitarianism*, rev. 1958

Between Past and Future: Six Exercises in Political Thought (New York, 1961; rev. edn with two additional essays, 1968)

Eichmann in Jerusalem: A Report on the Banality of Evil (New York, 1963, rev. 1965); trans. as *Eichmann in Jerusalem: Ein Bericht von der Banalität des Bösen* (Munich, 1964)

Über die Revolution (Munich, 1963); trans. as *On Revolution* (New York, 1963, rev. 1965)

Men in Dark Times (New York, 1968)

On Violence (New York, 1970); trans. as *Macht und Gewalt* (Munich, 1975)

Walter Benjamin–Bertolt Brecht: Zwei Essays (Munich, 1971) [previously
  included in *Men in Dark Times*]
Crises of the Republic (New York, 1972)
Wahrheit und Lüge in der Politik: Zwei Essays (Munich, 1972)
Die verborgene Tradition: Acht Essays (Frankfurt, 1976) [containd *Sechs Essays*
  (1948), 'Aufklärung und Judenfrage' (1932) and 'Zionism Reconsidered'
  (1945)]
The Jew as Pariah: Jewish Identity and Politics in the Modern Age, ed. and
  intro. Ron H. Feldman (New York, 1978)
The Life of the Mind, ed. Mary McCarthy (New York, 1978)
Lectures on Kant's Political Philosophy (Chicago, IL, 1982)
Ich selbst, auch ich tanze: Die Gedichte (Munich, 2015)

Edited by Hannah Arendt: English

Lazare, Bernard, *Job's Dungheap* (New York, 1948)
Jaspers, Karl, *The Great Philosophers*, vols I and II (New York, 1962–6)
Benjamin, Walter, *Illuminations*, trans. Harry Zohn (New York, 1968) [intro.
  repr. in *Men in Dark Times* (1968)]

Edited by Hannah Arendt: German

Broch, Hermann, *Dichten und Erkennen, Essays*, VI and VII of *Gesammelte
  Werke* (Zürich, 1955) [Arendt's intro., trans. Richard and Clara Winson,
  in *Men in Dark Times*]
Jaspers, Karl, *Wahrheit, Freiheit und Friede* (Munich, 1958) [intro. trans.,
  in *Men in Dark Times*]

Collected Essays, Interviews, Books, Reviews, Articles

Essays in Understanding, 1930–1954, ed. Jerome Kohn (New York, 1994)
Denktagebuch, 1950–1973, 2 vols (Munich, 2002)
Responsibility and Judgment, ed. Jerome Kohn (New York, 2003)
The Promise of Politics, ed. Jerome Kohn (New York, 2005)

The Jewish Writings, ed. Jerome Kohn and Ron H. Feldman (New York, 2007)
Reflections on Literature and Culture, ed. Susannah Young-Ah Gottlieb
    (Stanford, CA, 2007)
Thinking Without a Banister: Essays in Understanding, 1953–1975, ed. Jerome
    Kohn (New York, 2018)

Correspondence Published in English

Arendt, Hannah, and Karl Jaspers, *Correspondence, 1926–1969*, ed. Lotte
    Köhler and Hans Saner (New York, 1993)
*Between Friends: The Correspondence of Hannah Arendt and Mary McCarthy,
    1949–1975*, ed. Carol Brightman (New York, 1996)
*Within Four Walls: The Correspondence between Hannah Arendt and Heinrich
    Blücher, 1936–1968*, ed. Lotte Köhler (New York, 2000)
Arendt, Hannah, and Martin Heidegger, *Letters, 1925–1975*, ed. Ursula Ludz,
    trans. Andrew Shields (New York, 2003)
The Correspondence of Hannah Arendt and Gershom Scholem, ed. Marie Luise
    Knott, trans. Anthony David (Chicago, IL, 2017)

Correspondence Published in German

Arendt, Hannah, and Hermann Broch, *Briefwechsel, 1946 bis 1951*, ed. Paul
    Michael Lützeler (Berlin, 1996)
Arendt, Hannah, *Wie ich einmal ohne Dich leben soll, mag ich mir nicht
    vorstellen: Briefwechsel mit den Freundinnen Charlotte Beradt, Rose
    Feitelson, Hilde Fränkel, Anne Weil-Mendelsohn und Helen Wolff*, ed.
    Ursula Ludz and Ingeborg Nordmann (Munich, 2017)
Arendt, Hannah, and Günther Anders, *Schreib doch mal 'hard facts' über
    Dich: Briefe, 1939 bis 1975*, ed. Kerstin Putz (Munich, 2018)

Selected Books about Hannah Arendt

Benhabib, Seyla, *The Reluctant Modernism of Hannah Arendt* (Lanham, MD,
    2003)

——, *Politics in Dark Times: Encounters with Hannah Arendt* (Cambridge, 2010)

Bernstein, Richard J., *Hannah Arendt and the Jewish Question* (Cambridge, 1996)

——, *Why Read Hannah Arendt Now?* (Cambridge, 2018)

Canovan, Margaret, *The Political Thought of Hannah Arendt* (London, 1974)

Dietz, Mary, *Turning Operations: Feminism, Arendt, and Politics* (New York and London, 2002)

Disch, Lisa, *Hannah Arendt and the Limits of Philosophy* (Ithaca, NY, 1994)

Gines, Kathryn T., *Hannah Arendt and the Negro Question* (Bloomington, IN, 2014)

Honig, Bonnie, *Feminist Interpretations of Hannah Arendt* (University Park, PA, 1994)

Isaac, Jeffrey, *Arendt, Camus, and Modern Rebellion* (New Haven, CT, 1992)

Kateb, George, *Hannah Arendt: Politics, Conscience, Evil* (Oxford, 1984)

May, Larry, and Jerome Kohn, *Hannah Arendt: Twenty Years Later* (Cambridge, MA, 1996)

Pitkin, Hannah, *The Attack of the Blob: Hannah Arendt's Concept of the Social* (Chicago, IL, 1998)

Villa, Dana, *Arendt and Heidegger: The Fate of the Political* (Princeton, NJ, 1996)

——, *The Cambridge Companion to Hannah Arendt* (Cambridge, 2000)

Young-Bruehl, Elisabeth, *Hannah Arendt: For Love of the World* [1982] (New Haven, CT, 2004)

——, *Why Arendt Matters* (New Haven, CT, 2006)

Acknowledgements

Writing an introductory biography of Hannah Arendt's life and work has been a tremendous endeavour. When I appeared in the world Hannah Arendt was already gone, and so I have come to know her through her writing, the work of others and those who knew her. This has been no easy task, and it would not have been possible without the hard work, kindness and guidance of those who came before me. Much of the detail in this biography, especially concerning the early years of Arendt's life, would not exist without Elisabeth Young-Bruehl's *For the Love of the World*. And I'm quite certain none of this would exist at all if it were not for Jerome Kohn, who preserves the work and legacy of Hannah Arendt.

Without the dedicated work of librarians and archivists, this would be a much poorer text. I am forever grateful to Barbara Bair, who oversees the Hannah Arendt Archive at the Library of Congress in Washington, DC, for letting me handle Arendt's papers. Because of Ulrich von Bullow, I was able to read Arendt's thinking journals in the German Literature Archive in Marbach, Germany, which opened Arendt's thinking to me in an entirely new way. Helene Tieger stands guard over Hannah Arendt's Library at the Stevenson Library and has given me the immense pleasure of wandering aimlessly through Arendt's stacks. Some of the more intimate details I've been able to include about Arendt's immigration and friendships were found in The Berg Collection and Manuscript Reading Room at the New York Public Library. And thank you to the staff at the Bodleian in special collections who, due to unusual circumstances, were able to send me the final documents I needed to finish writing.

For the past six years I have been teaching courses on Hannah Arendt at the Brooklyn Institute for Social Research in New York City. My students, willing test subjects, unknowingly allowed me to work out my ideas for this book in the classroom. And to my friends and colleagues at the Brooklyn Institute, who have given me a sense of home in the world, free to pursue the life of the mind without the constraints of academia: Suzanne Schneider, Ajay Sign Chaudhary, Mark DeLucas – thank you.

To my other intellectual home, the Quite tribe at Bard College – you know who you are.

Thank you with love to my Heidelberg family, Laurie Grace King and Kim Berly for good, old-fashioned fun. Laurie, I don't know what the world would be without you. You are my Hilde Frankel. And to the generous baristas at Coffee Nerd for letting me sit endlessly while, over the past six years, I wrote a dissertation and two books upstairs.

Endless thanks are due to my ever-patient editors Vivian Constantinopoulos and Phoebe Colley. Many thanks as well to Benjamin Wurgaft, who read an early draft with a critical eye and his keen sense of humour, and John D. Macready, for his conversation and consultation. Michael Stevenson was kind enough to look over my writing on Heidegger – thank you for being there. I had the great fortune to visit with Richard Bernstein at the New School for Social Research, who brought Arendt to life for me with his stories, and the inestimable gift of Jerome Kohn's edits on the final draft. And thank you to Lyndsey Stonebridge for recommending I write this book.

As Hannah Arendt well knew, writing requires one retreat from the world of appearances to the realm of solitude. Thank you to my friends and family who continuously put up with my long and unpredictable absences: Susan Gillespie, Mark Gutzmer, Klara Zwickl, Dad, Mom, Eli, Scott, Alexandra, Lee, Sophia, Jackson, Christopher, Vivian, Ruth, Isabel Rose Sutherby Hill – I love you all.

Thomas Luke Bartscherer, these visions of Johanna are for you. *Amo: Volo ut sis.*

Photo Acknowledgements

Adoc-photos/Art Resource, NY: p. 114; © Estate of Fred Stein/BPK Bildagentur/Art Resource, NY: p. 6; © Estate of Gisèle Freund/Institut Mémoires de l'édition contemporaine (IMEC), Fonds MCC, Dist. RMN-Grand Palais/Art Resource, NY: p. 94; courtesy of the Hannah Arendt Bluecher Literary Trust/Art Resource, NY: pp. 18, 19, 20, 24, 26, 27, 29, 30, 35, 37, 49, 56, 62, 68, 72, 73, 79, 104, 108, 109, 117, 135, 155, 172, 189, 190, 193, 196, 198, 205.